Herrn Professor W. Heissig
in Freundschaft
von N. Poppe

LANGUAGE HANDBOOK SERIES : Frank A. Rice, General Editor

MONGOLIAN

LANGUAGE HANDBOOK

NICHOLAS POPPE

CENTER FOR APPLIED LINGUISTICS : 1970

INTRODUCTION TO THE SERIES

Each volume in the Language Handbook Series is intended to provide
an outline of the salient features of a particular language and a
summary of the language situation and language problems of the
country or area in which it is spoken. The scope of the series is
the major modern languages of Asia and Africa.

It is hoped that the handbooks will prove useful to several
different kinds of readers. One is the linguistic specialist who
is not himself a specialist in the particular language treated,
e.g. a Swahili scholar who is interested in Arabic. Another is
the student who is past the beginning stages of his study and who
wishes to have a concise and condensed general picture of the language and its setting. A third reader is the area specialist,
e.g. a sociologist, who wishes to know basic linguistic or socio-
linguistic facts about the area. The handbooks are not designed
to serve as instructional materials for the language in question,
nor are they intended as a guide to local customs or cultural
differences or the like.

There has been some attempt to hold the handbooks to a sug-
gested general framework so as to give the series some uniformity,
but in practice the individual studies vary considerably, both
because of the differences of approach of the individual authors
and the range and variety of problems of the individual languages.
In general, each author in his own way treats the following matters:
the language in its social and historical setting, its linguistic
structure, its writing system (as appropriate), its points of contrast with English, and its literature. The description of the
linguistic structure has provided the greatest problem in presen-
tation. The authors have made a serious effort to avoid excessive
use of technical linguistic terminology but nevertheless a certain
amount of linguistic sophistication on the part of the reader must
be assumed. Given the status of modern linguistics as a discipline

it has not seemed wise to attempt to write in a popularized style.

The language handbooks represent a new kind of venture in the field of applied linguistics. It is probable that some portions or aspects of the various studies will be found inadequate or of little value, but the authors and the editor are confident that the series as a whole represents a useful step in the application of linguistic knowledge to practical language problems.

Frank A. Rice
Director, Office of Information and Publications
Center for Applied Linguistics

MONGOLIAN LANGUAGE HANDBOOK

PREFACE

The present book is an introduction to Mongolian and is designed to give the most essential information about that language to nonspecialists in the field, primarily to linguists who are interested in learning about the structure of Mongolian, or students of Mongolian who wish to get a general picture of the language before they begin studying it in detail. General readers interested in languages may also find this book useful.

This is not a textbook for the study of the Mongolian language. In a textbook, grammatical rules are frequently distributed among the various lessons, in connection with illustrative exercises. The present book, however, provides a systematic discussion of the phonology, morphology, and syntax, and gives the necessary information about each of these in one place. As a result, this book may be useful to the student of Mongolian who wishes to review and systematize his knowledge of Mongolian grammar.

In comparison to many other languages, Mongolian has been little studied, and there is even confusion with regard to the term "Mongolian." Therefore, the reader is asked to pay particular attention to what is said in sections 1.2 and 1.3 about the Mongolian language and the Mongolian language family. The present book is primarily concerned with the Mongolian language, and the information supplied is based on Khalkha, the main dialect spoken in the Mongolian People's Republic, which is easily understood by all Mongols who inhabit the Republic and those who inhabit Inner Mongolia, i.e. Chinese Mongolia.

The insufficient knowledge of, and the misconceptions about, the Mongols and Mongolia, so characteristic of most of the nonspecialists in the Mongolian field, have been taken into account, and therefore the most essential geographic and historical information is also given here.

PREFACE

The Mongols have an old and relatively rich literature.
A brief sketch of their literature, including folklore, follows
the linguistic sections of this book.

The main source for the present book is the author's
Khalkha-Mongolische Grammatik (1951), but J.C. Street's Khalkha
Structure (1963), S. Luvsanvandan's Mongol xèlnii züïn surax
bičig 1-2 (Ulaanbaatar, 1956), and Orčin cagiïn mongol xèlnii
züï (Ulaanbaatar, 1957) were also used.

Nicholas Poppe

NOTATIONS

Mongolian words, phrases, and clauses are given either in phonemic transcription (2.1) or in transliteration (1.8). Where
it is necessary a phonetic transcription is enclosed within
square brackets.

SYMBOLS

/ /	encloses phonemic transcription
[ ]	encloses phonetic transcription
' '	encloses glosses or translations
___	underlines transliteration
-	at the end of a sequence indicates a verb stem; before a suffix, indicates that the suffix is taken by verbs; before and after a suffix, indicates that the suffix is added to verb stems and forms verb stems
+	at the end of a sequence indicates a noun stem; before a suffix, indicates that the suffix is added to noun stems; between two sequences, indicates internal open juncture
*	indicates a reconstructed or hypothetical form
<	indicates direction of development ('developed from...' or 'originated from...')
>	indicates direction of development ('developed to...' or 'yielded...')
~	'alternates with'

TABLE OF CONTENTS

TABLE OF CONTENTS

1. THE LANGUAGE SITUATION

1.1. What is Mongolian?

Mongolian is the speech of members of an ethnic group living in
various regions of Central Asia, in the adjacent parts of Manchuria and East Siberia, in Northern Tibet, in some areas of
Afghanistan, and as far west as the Lower Volga region in the
European part of the USSR. It is only natural that the Mongols,
being scattered over such a vast area, do not have a uniform
language. Instead, they speak a large number of dialects, some
of which are so different from other dialects that their speakers are not understood by Mongols of other areas. For this
reason such dialects are considered different, although mutually
related, languages.

The various Mongolian languages have different names, and
only one is called Mongolian. There are nine other languages,
namely, Buriat, Dagur, Monguor, Santa, Paongan, Yellow Uighur,
Moghol, Oirat, and Kalmyk (see Table 1).

1.2. The Mongolian language

The Mongolian language is spoken in the Mongolian People's
Republic (MPR), in the adjacent parts of Manchuria, and in an
area called Inner Mongolia (IM). Both Inner Mongolia and Manchuria are at present part of China. The language as spoken in
the three areas is only more or less uniform. The native speakers
of the various dialects of the Mongolian language (see Table 2)
understand each other as easily as the native speakers of English
whose homes are in different parts of England or America. A Mongol from the MPR converses with a Mongol from Inner Mongolia as
easily as an Englishman from Middlesex understands an American
from New York or a Canadian from British Columbia.

1

Table 1

The Mongolian languages

	Language	Known number of speakers	Geographic distribution
1.	Mongolian	1,639,100 (1959)	See Section 1.2.
2.	Buriat	253,000 (1959) 24,000 (1956)	Autonomous Buriat Republic; autonomous districts in the Irkutsk and Chita regions of the USSR; northern MPR; and an unknown number in northwestern Manchuria
3.	Oirat	60,000 (1956)	Northwestern MPR; an unspecified number in the Autonomous Uighur District in Sinkiang (China); and in the Kuku Nor region in the Ch'inghai province of China
4.	Kalmyk	106,000 (1959)	Kalmyk Autonomous Republic in the USSR
5.	Moghol	————	Various places in the provinces of Herāt, Maimana, and Badakhshān of Afghanistan
6.	Dagur	22,600 (1953- 2,000 1954)	Northwestern Manchuria and Chuguchak district, province of Sinkiang, China
7.	Monguor	53,000 (1953- 1954)	Parts of the provinces of Kansu and Ch'inghai in China
8.	Santa	155,500 (1953- 1954)	Parts of the province of Kansu in China
9.	Paongan	8,000 (1953- 1954)	Vicinity of Paongan, province of Ch'inghai in China
10.	Yellow Uighur	1,200 (1954)	Kan-chou in the province of Kansu in China

Note: The figures enclosed in parentheses indicate the year of the census. The first figure for speakers of Buriat refers to the USSR, the second figure refers to the MPR. The first figure for speakers of Dagur refers to Manchuria, the second figure refers to the Chuguchak district.

THE LANGUAGE SITUATION

The total number of speakers of the Mongolian language
amounts to approximately 1,639,100 persons. Of these, 655,100
live in the MPR, and the remaining one million or so live in
Manchuria and Inner Mongolia.

The most important dialect of the Mongolian language is
Khalkha, which is spoken by the majority of the population of
the MPR. It is the official language of the nation, the total
population of which amounts to 845,500 persons (1956 census) and
comprises a number of Mongolian ethnic subgroups, each speaking
a separate dialect or language; see Table 3.

The dialects of these eight ethnic subgroups are named after
the subgroups, i.e. the Khalkha dialect, the Dariganga dialect,
etc. Of these eight different dialects, Khalkha and Dariganga
are dialects of the Mongolian language. Buriat is an independent
language -- not a dialect of the Mongolian language. Dialects
nos. 4 through 8 are dialects of the Oirat language. The remaining ethnic subgroups of the population of the MPR are Kazakhs and
Uriankha, both speaking two different Turkic languages. There
are also Russians, Chinese, Evenki (Tungus), and representatives
of other non-Mongolian peoples.

The literary language in use in the Mongolian People's Republic is based on Khalkha. It serves all groups of Mongols
living in the MPR, i.e. 742,600 persons. According to the census
of 1956, the total number of literate Mongols was close to 500,000.

The alphabet is Cyrillic. It was introduced in 1941. Until
then, the old alphabet of Uighur origin was used, and the written
language was an archaic form of Mongolian, going back to the
thirteenth century and very different from spoken Mongolian (see
1.7.)

There is an extensive literature and press in the new literary language. For example, in 1960 there existed 29 newspapers,
with a combined annual circulation of 11,816,800 copies, and 16
periodicals, with a combined annual circulation of 2,394,500
copies.

Table 2

The main dialects of the Mongolian language

Name of the dialect	Number of speakers	Geographical distribution
Khalkha	639,100	Mongolian People's Republic
Dariganga	16,000	Southeastern MPR
Chakhar	unspecified	Chakhar district, IM
Urat	unspecified	Ulan Tsab district, IM
Kharchin-Tümüt	± 300,000	Jou Uda district, IM
Khorchin	unspecified	Jerim district, IM
Üjümüchin	unspecified	Shilingol district, IM, and in the MPR where there are emigrants from Shilingol
Ordos	unspecified	Yeke Juu district, IM
Bargu	unspecified	Khulun-Buyir district, N.W. Manchuria

Note: The dialects of the Mongolian language are not denoted on the map facing page 1.

In 1960 there were 419 elementary schools, 15 high schools, and 7 institutions of higher education at the university level. The number of students in that year was 131,046, including 6,909 university students.

The Khalkha dialect and the literary language which is based on it are easily understood by all speakers of the Mongolian language, no matter what their dialect may be.

1.3. The Mongolian language family

As has been indicated, the Mongolian language is not an isolated language, but a member of a group of related languages. The family of Mongolian languages (see Table 1) comprises the Mongolian language (including all its dialects) and nine other languages, most of which are as incomprehensible to the speakers of the Mongolian language as German is to an Englishman who has never studied it. Nevertheless, the Mongolian languages are related languages, with mutual relations comparable to those of the Germanic languages.

The total known number of speakers of Mongolian languages is estimated at 2,262,400. It is probably safe to assume that the actual number of speakers is closer to 3 million.

1.4. Linguistic classification

The Mongolian languages belong to the so-called Altaic language group, which comprises the Mongolian, Turkic, Manchu-Tungus languages, and, according to some scholars, also Korean. The Turkic languages are: Turkish, spoken in Turkey; Azerbaijani; Turkmen; Uzbek; Kazakh; Kirghiz; Tatar; and many other languages. Manchu is a written language. It is spoken by a small group of people in Manchuria. Tungus comprises Evenki, Lamut, Negidal, Solon, and a few other minor languages spoken in East Siberia. Korean is the language spoken in Korea.

The Altaic languages have many features in common. All of them are agglutinative, i.e. word-formation and inflection are

5

Table 3

The ethnic composition of the Mongolian population of the MPR

	Name of the subgroup	Total number	Percentage of the total population of the MPR
1.	Khalkha	639,100	75.6%
2.	Dariganga	16,000	2.0
3.	Buriat	24,600	2.9
4.	Dörbet	25,700	3.0
5.	Bayit	15,900	1.9
6.	Dzakhachin	10,800	1.3
7.	Öölet	4,900	0.6
8.	Torguut	4,700	0.5

carried out by adding of suffixes to otherwise unchanging word-stems, e.g. Mong.[san-], stem of the verb "to think", in [san-ǎn] 'he thinks', [san-ǎw] 'he thought', [san-ā] 'the thought'; Turk. [er] 'man', [er+lär] 'men'; [gel-], stem of the verb "to come", in [gel-iyor] 'he comes', [gel-di] 'he came', etc.

Another characteristic feature is the nominal character of the verb, i.e. the verbal forms have originated from nouns, cf. Mong. naɣad-, stem of the verb "to play": naɣad-u-m 'the play' and 'he plays'; Turk. ač-, stem of the verb "to open": ač-ar 'key' and 'he will open'.

The Altaic languages also have a common vocabulary. A large number of regular sound correspondences has been established, and there is much in favor of the assumption that the Altaic languages are genetically related to each other, although some scholars doubt it and regard all common elements in vocabulary and grammar as criss-cross borrowings which occurred at different times. How-ever, if there is a genetic affinity between the Altaic languages,

Mongolian must be regarded as related to Turkish or Evenki, much as English, being a Germanic language, is related to Polish, which is a Slavic language, both Germanic and Slavic belonging to the Indo-European language family.

1.5. Historical background

The Mongols are first mentioned in historical documents of the eighth century A.D. At that time, one of their major tribes, the Tatars, was known, but the name "Mongol" occurs for the first time in the period of the Chinese T'ang dynasty (A.D. 618-907). Most of what is Mongolia today was then inhabited by Turks, and the Mongolian tribes lived in Northwestern Manchuria and in the southern part of Transbaikalia, i.e. the region to the east of Lake Baikal in Siberia.

The first ruler of a relatively large federation of the Mongols was Khaidu who in the eleventh century united a number of tribes. That federation was called "Mongol". At that time, the Turks had already moved to the west, and most of their former territory was populated by various Mongolian tribes. The federation reached its highest power under Khaidu's grandson, Khabul. After his death, the federation declined. Temüjin (born ca. 1155), who later assumed the title Chingis Khan, united the Mongolian tribes again, restored the old name Mongol, and became the founder of a vast Mongolian empire. The empire was proclaimed in 1206. It comprised most of the present territories of the Mongolian People's Republic, Inner Mongolia, Transbaikalia, and the northwestern part of Manchuria. Chingis Khan began the conquest of North China and undertook several military campaigns against Tangut (a principality inhabited by a people related to the Tibetans), but paid most of his attention to the conquest of what is now Chinese and Russian Turkestan. Chingis Khan's vanguard armies moved around the Caspian Sea and converged in Southern Russia, where, on May 31, 1222, they inflicted an overwhelming defeat upon the Russians. After the completion of the

conquest of Turkestan, in 1225, Chingis Khan returned to Mongolia.
He died in 1227, during his last campaign in Tangut, and was suc-
ceeded by his son Ögedei, who ruled from 1229 to 1241. During his
reign, the conquest of North China was completed and the ruling
dynasty, Kin (1125-1234), fell. Subsequently, war was waged
against South China, which was under the rule of the Sung dynasty
(960-1279). However, the greatest conquests were made in the
West. All of Southern Russia and large areas of Middle Russia
were occupied, and Kiev, the oldest city in Russia and her former
capital, was captured and destroyed in 1240. The Mongolian army,
which included soldiers of many other nationalities, also invaded
Poland, Silesia, Austria, and Hungary, under the command of Batu,
a grandson of Chingis Khan. When the news of Ögedei's death
reached him, Batu withdrew his armed forces and went back to
Mongolia, and the Mongols never returned to the regions west of
Russia. But Russia remained under Mongolian domination for a
long time. Eastern Russia, at that time inhabited mostly by
Finno-Ugric and Turkic tribes, became a Mongolian vassal kingdom
in 1237, which continued in power under the name of the Golden
Horde until 1438, when it split into two kingdoms. One of these,
the Kazan Kingdom, was later, in 1552, conquered by the Russian
Tsar Ivan IV. The territory of the Golden Horde was populated by
Turks and other non-Mongolian tribes. There were very few Mongols in the territory, and the Mongolian language was not spoken
after 1325. Only one event connected with the Mongolian conquests
in the West is important from the linguistic point of view. This
is Hülegü's campaign against Afghanistan. Hülegü, with an army
of 129,000, set off to conquer Persia and other countries of
Western Asia. In the course of this military enterprise he invaded Afghanistan and set up Mongolian garrisons. The descendants of the soldiers stationed there are the Moghols of our time.
Thus, a new ethnic group and a new language appeared as a result
of the Mongolian wars.

The population of the Mongolian Empire at the time of Chingis
Khan and Ögedei included many Mongolian tribes and clans whose

names still exist, such as Khori Tümet, who are identified with
the Khori, the name of a Buriat tribe. Another tribe mentioned
in the thirteenth and fourteenth centuries is Ikires, which is
identical with the present-day Ekhirit, also a Buriat tribe.
The Oirat, Jalayir, Sünit, and other tribes which still exist
were mentioned in various sources of the thirteenth and fourteenth centuries. The foundation of the Mongolian Empire and
the subsequent wars played an important role in the development
of the Mongolian languages. Military service and the numerous
campaigns reshuffled the Mongolian clans and tribes, regrouped
them, and united them.

The Mongolian Empire experienced its greatest expansion
under Khubilai Khan (1259-1294). His armies conquered the remaining part of China and he founded a new capital at a location
near the present city of Peking. Under him, a new dynasty was
proclaimed, named Yüan, which remained in power until 1368. His
realm was no longer an empire of the Mongols, but became a Sino-
Mongolian Empire, in which the Mongols were a small minority
among China's vast population. The center of political life
shifted from Mongolia to China, and the original Mongolian territories became a remote borderland which played no role in the
political, economic, and cultural life of the Empire.

When the Yüan dynasty collapsed in 1368 and the last Yüan
emperor fled to Mongolia, China came under native Chinese rulers,
the Ming dynasty (1368-1644). In Mongolia, internal feuds soon
began and continued intermittently until the end of the seventeenth century. During this period of more than 300 years, the
political power shifted several times from the Mongolian princes
to the Oirat rulers. The Mongols were united again for a short
time under Dayan Khan (1470-1543). After his death, the Khalkha
region, which represents approximately four-fifths of the present
territory of the Mongolian People's Republic, became a separate
principality. It had been bequeathed by Dayan to his youngest
son, Geresenje. At a later period, in 1635, Southern Mongolia,
i.e. the country to the south of Khalkha, was conquered by the

Manchus, who also conquered all of China, proclaimed their dynasty (Tai Ch'ing [1644-1911]), and made Southern Mongolia an integral part of China. This gave rise to the terms "Inner Mongolia" and "Outer Mongolia". Inner Mongolia belonged to China and was, so to speak, within its national boundaries, whereas Outer Mongolia (Khalkha) remained for a while independent, and was outside the Chinese territory.

In the seventeenth century, many important events took place. First of all, the feuds of the Mongolian princes still continued. The most devastating war was that waged upon the Mongols by the Oirat prince Galdan Bushuktu in 1688. It caused a mass flight of the Mongols across the northern frontier into the land of the Buriats. The war was so disastrous to the Mongols that their princes had to ask the Tai Ch'ing Emperor to intervene. In return, they pledged allegiance to the Tai Ch'ing dynasty (but not to China). As a result, Outer Mongolia became a dependency of the Manchu-Chinese Empire in 1691.

Also in the seventeenth century, the Buriats, who lived in East Siberia in the regions west, south, and east of Lake Baikal, were conquered by the Russians and became Russian subjects. Soon Russian settlers appeared, and the first cities were built. This was the beginning of Russian cultural and linguistic influence upon the Buriats.

The seventeenth century was also the period of the Oirat migrations. Originally -- at the time of Chingis Khan -- the Oirats lived on the upper course of the Yenisei River, but in the seventeenth century their center was in Jungaria, the northwestern part of the Sinkiang province in China. Their life was anything but peaceful because of the wars between the Oirat princes and frequent raids by Kazakhs. In 1606, one of their princes, Kho Örlük, opened negotiations with the Russian authorities, and soon a large group of Oirats under his leadership left Jungaria and moved into the Volga region. They arrived there in 1630. Their descendants, known as the Kalmyks, are still there, and the Kalmyk language came into existence as the result of the separation

10

of its speakers from the other Oirats. However, some of the
Kalmyks left Russia in 1771 and returned to Jungaria. Some of
the Oirats moved, in the seventeenth century, into the region
west of Khalkha, i.e. into the territory of the present-day
districts Bayan Ölegei, Ubsa Nuur, and Kobdo of the MPR. Their
descendants are still there. Another group of Oirats migrated
into the Kuku Nor region, Ch'inghai, and some of them settled in
the valley of the river Etsin Gol. Consequently, the Oirats are
widely scattered.

The seventeenth century was also the period of the rapid
spread of Lamaism, a relatively new form of Buddhism. All the
Mongols, both in Inner and Outer Mongolia, the Oirats (including
the Kalmyks), and some of the Buriats became Buddhists, either
in the seventeenth century or at the beginning of the eighteenth
century. Buddhism brought learning, and the only schools that
existed were in monasteries. The monasteries also engaged in
extensive literary activity. Numerous Buddhist books were translated from Tibetan into Mongolian, and a large number of them
were published by the monasteries.

The seventeenth century was also the time of appearance of
political boundaries separating various groups of Mongols. Inner
Mongolia became an integral part of China, and the Mongols in
Manchuria became subjects of China also. Outer Mongolia remained
a semi-independent country, but was still a Chinese protectorate.
The Buriats and Kalmyks became subjects of Russia. In addition,
there were minor groups of Mongols in Afghanistan and in various
areas of China.

For a number of reasons the seventeenth century was also an
important period in the history of the Mongolian language. It
was the beginning of the "New Mongolian" period, and likewise the
time of the appearance of the Oirat script, devised in 1648 by
the learned lama Zaya Pandita, and of the Oirat written language.

The subsequent periods were relatively quiet. Under the
rule of the Tai Ch'ing dynasty, Inner Mongolia and Manchuria
underwent extensive colonization by Chinese farmers. In many

areas the Mongols lost their livelihood, because no place was
left to them where they could graze their cattle. In most regions
of Inner Mongolia the Mongols became a minority group, the main
population being Chinese. At the present time, the population of
Inner Mongolia amounts to 7,400,000 persons. The total number of
Mongols in China is 1,463,000, of whom 997,000 live in the Autonomous Inner Mongolian Region.

In Outer Mongolia the activities of the Chinese merchants
and usurers ruined thousands of nomads. High taxes and the corvée
system imposed by the Mongolian princes, enormous tributes paid to
the Imperial court in Peking, mismanagement and corruption of of-
ficials, injustice, and disregard for human rights, all created
discontent among the Mongols of Outer Mongolia. As a result,
rebellions occurred. One rebellion, led by the Oirat Amur Sanaa,
engulfed most of Outer Mongolia and lasted from 1754 to 1758.
A rebellion of the Moslems, in the second half of the nineteenth
century, lasted many years and was particularly ruinous to the
Mongols.

In China, the revolution of 1911 that resulted in the overthrow of the Tai Ch'ing dynasty was favorable to the Mongol's
aspirations for national liberation. The Mongols declared Outer
Mongolia an independent nation. Their autonomy was recognized
by China and Russia in 1913, and a special joint declaration was
issued to that effect. In spite of the fact that this declaration still recognized the suzerainty of China over Outer Mongolia,
the latter preserved its semi-independent status until the revolution of 1917 in Russia. The fall of the Tsarist government,
and the annulment by the Soviet government of all treaties con-
cluded by the old regime, were taken advantage of by the Chinese
authorities, who in 1919 sent an occupation army into Mongolia.
In the meantime, civil war was ravaging the former Russian Empire.
One of the anti-communist military leaders, Baron Ungern-Sternberg,
retreated with his military forces from Siberia to Outer Mongolia,
in order to regroup. There he defeated the Chinese, expelled them
from Mongolia, and helped the Mongols to re-establish their own

government, which was headed by the religious leader of Mongolia,
the Jebtsun Damba Khutuktu, who assumed the title of Emperor.
Baron Ungern-Sternberg's army, defeated in several encounters
with the Soviet Red army, was demoralized and soon fell apart.
It dissolved into numerous bands which confiscated food and horses
from the Mongols, and even attacked the population. Finally, in
1921 the Mongolian government permitted the Soviet armed forces
to enter Mongolia and liquidate the remaining groups of the former
White army. In 1921, a People's Government was established, and
after the death of Jebtsun Damba Khutuktu in 1924, Outer Mongolia
was proclaimed a People's Republic. According to its constitu-
tion, it was a nation which was planned to develop according to
the non-capitalistic way, and the foundation for a gradual tran-
sition to socialism was envisioned.

During the less than fifty years of Outer Mongolia's independence, great changes have occurred in her economic, social,
and cultural life. The cultural changes are of particular im-
portance because the spread of education, the opening of various
types of schools, including universities, the coming into existence of an academy of sciences and other learned bodies, the
large circulation of books and periodicals, regular radio broad-
casting, and the introduction of television, have all raised the
cultural level enormously and produced great changes in the language, which is constantly being enriched by new words and terminology.

Similar great changes have occurred in the Buriat and Kalmyk
areas, two autonomous republics within the USSR, where literacy
is now almost 100 percent.

As for Inner Mongolia, not much is known about recent developments, or about the general position of the Mongols. It is
known that they still use the old Mongolian alphabet, which was
abolished in 1931 in the Buriat Republic and in 1941 in the MPR.
There is a Mongolian university in Kuku Khoto (Kweisui, in Chinese).
Otherwise nothing is known about the linguistic situation or the
general cultural conditions in Inner Mongolia.

1.6. Historical periods of the language

The time of the first appearance of the oldest form of Mongolian
is unknown, but what is called "Ancient Mongolian" (AMo.) probably lasted until the twelfth century A.D., i.e. until the first
federations of the Mongolian tribes were established. Ancient
Mongolian has not been preserved in written sources, and the only
material available is a few words attested in Chinese annals and
a number of words borrowed by the ancestors of the present-day
Tungus from Ancient Mongolian, e.g. Evenki atiga 'knapsack'
< AMo. *atigā > Kh. ačaa [ač^hā] 'load transported on horseback',
which has preserved the consonant *t before i, and the consonant
*g in intervocalic position before a long vowel.

At the end of the Ancient Mongolian period, the old Mongolian script and the so-called Script Mongolian language appeared. Although Script Mongolian has preserved a few AMo.
features, such as intervocalic *g, it is not identical with AMo.
and represents a stage transitional to Middle Mongolian.

Middle Mongolian is the language that was spoken from the
twelfth century to the sixteenth or even seventeenth century.
At that time, the language still preserved the initial h in words
such as harban 'ten' = Kh. arav [arwǎ], but intervocalic *g had
already disappeared, e.g. ba'u- 'to descend' (AMo. *bagū-) = Kh.
buu- [Bū-]. This stage is represented by the language of the
so-called Secret History, a work written in the thirteenth century and preserved in Chinese phonetic transcription. Other
sources are various Chinese-Mongolian glossaries of the fourteenth century, edicts and other texts written in the so-called
'Phags-pa Script (1269-1368), and Mongolian-Arabic and Persian-
Mongolian glossaries and dictionaries of the thirteenth and fourteenth centuries, in which Mongolian is rendered with Arabic
letters. There are also lists of words in Georgian and Armenian
transcription, and individual words in Latin transcription which
are found in diaries of the European travelers who visited Mongolia in the thirteenth and fourteenth centuries.

The Middle Mongolian Period was followed by the "New Mongolian" Period. Only after the seventeenth century did Mongolian, Buriat, Oirat, and Kalmyk acquire their characteristic features and gradually become what they are at the present time.

The most recent period of the Mongolian language history began in the 1920's, after revolutions had occurred in China, Russia, and Mongolia, in a period during which political, economic, social, and cultural changes took place.

1.7. The old Mongolian scripts

The earliest written record of the Mongolian language is an inscription on a stele erected in honor of Chingis Khan's nephew, Yisünke. The inscription, which can be dated approximately A.D. 1225, shows an orthography which closely corresponds to the orthography of later periods, which suggests that the script was established prior to that date.

The Old Mongolian script is of Uighur origin. The Uighurs were a Turkic nation with a relatively high civilization, and possessed a script from the time of the seventh century A.D. Their most ancient kingdom was in the ninth century, in Mongolia. Later they moved to the West and established a kingdom in Chinese Turkestan. The Uighurs borrowed their script from the Sogdians, a civilized nation speaking an Iranian language. The Sogdian script is ultimately of Aramaic origin, and goes back to a North Semitic alphabet.

The Old Mongolian script is written vertically downwards, the columns running from left to right. This alphabet was used by all Mongols, including some of the Oirats, from the thirteenth century until recently.

The Buriats were the first to abolish the Old Mongolian script. They introduced the Latin alphabet in 1931, but replaced it in 1937 with the Russian alphabet. In the Mongolian People's Republic the old alphabet was in use until 1941, when it was also replaced by the Russian alphabet. The Mongols in Inner Mongolia still use the old alphabet.

Table 4

The letters of the Old Mongolian alphabet

Transcription	Characters		
	Initial	Medial	Final
a			
e			
i			
o u			
ö ü			
n			
ng			
q			
γ			
b			
p			
s			
š			
t d			
l			
m			
č			
ǰ			
y			
k g			
k			
r			
v			
h			

The Mongolian written in the old alphabet is called "Script Mongolian". It is based upon a dialect of the twelfth or early thirteenth century, a dialect which still retained some Ancient Mongolian features, but otherwise displayed Middle Mongolian forms. For example, it retained the intervocalic *ɣ before an original long vowel, e.g. baɣu- 'to descend' = Kh. buu- [Bū̬-]. On the other hand, it did not preserve the initial *p or *f or even its Middle Mongolian reflex, h; cf. arban 'ten' = MMo. harban = Kh. arav [arwǎ]; odun 'star' = MMo. hodun = Kh. od [ɔDDŏ].

Script Mongolian was used only as the language of writing; it was not a spoken language. It is phonologically and grammatically very different from Modern Mongolian. The following example will illustrate the difference:

Script Mongolian: baraɣun qoyina-ača bögen egülen ɣarču udal ügei sirügün boroɣan oroba

Modern Mongolian: baruun xoinoos böön üül garč udal-güi širüün boroo orov

Translation: 'There appeared from the northwest cumulus clouds, and soon a heavy rain fell'

The Old Mongolian alphabet has 24 letters. Each letter appears in three different forms, according to its position in the word: an initial one used at the beginning of words, a medial one used in the middle of words, and a final one used at the end of words. The letters of the Mongolian alphabet are given in Table 4.

The Emperor Khubilai of the Yüan dynasty conceived the plan of introducing another alphabet which would be suitable for all the languages spoken in his empire, including Chinese. The new script was invented by the learned Buddhist monk, 'Phags-pa Lama. It is based upon the Tibetan alphabet, and is called the "'Phags-pa Script", after its inventor. Sometimes it is referred to as the Square Script, because of the quadrangular shape of the letters. It was introduced in 1269, but used only until 1368. There are

Table 5

The vowel letters of the 'Phags-pa Script

ꑺ	—	a
ꑇ ꑇ	∧ ↑	o
ꑖ	ꑘ	u
ꑋ	ꑋ	e
ꑡ ꑡ	ꑤ ꑤ	ė
ꑥ ꑥ	ꑦ ꑦ	ö
ꑧ	ꑨ	ü
ꑩ	ꑩ	i

Table 6

The consonant letters of the 'Phags-pa Script

ᄅ	p	쥬	$\check{c}^{\prime}$
ᄅ	b	ᄐ	$\check{j}$
ᄃ 뗘	v	ᄀ	$\check{s}$
ᄝ	m	ᄝ	$\check{z}$
ᄐ	t	ᄬ	y
ᄌ	$t^{\prime}$	ᄁ	k
ᄂ	d	ᄫ	$k^{\prime}$
ᄋ	n	ᄘ	g
ᄑ	r	ᄆ	q
ᄅ	l	ᄖ	γ
ᄌ ᄌ	$c^{\prime}$	ᄅ	η
ᄆ ᄆ	j	ᄰ	h
ᄌ	s	ᄅ	$\cdot$
ᄐ	z	ᄃ	^{y}
ᄅ	$\check{c}$	◢	$\underset{\wedge}{u}$

few documents written in the 'Phags-pa Script, among which are
several imperial edicts, a Buddhist inscription, fragments of a
printed book, etc. The 'Phags-pa Script is shown in Tables 5
and 6.

1.8. The Cyrillic alphabet

Cyrillic is the name of the alphabets of Slavs of the Orthodox
Church. The Russian, Ukrainian, Bielorussian, Bulgarian, and
Serbian alphabets have developed from it, and are referred to as
Cyrillic.

The Cyrillic alphabet was introduced into the Mongolian
People's Republic in 1941. It consists of 34 letters. Of these,
32 are identical with the letters of the present-day Russian
alphabet, with two letters taken from the old Russian alphabet
(see Table 7). The Buriats and the Kalmyks also use alphabets
based upon the Russian alphabet, but they are slightly different
from the new Mongolian alphabet.

The relation between the letters and phonemes, and the ortho-
graphic rules will be explained below (see 2.4.).

Table 7

The new Mongolian (Cyrillic) alphabet

Letter	Latin Transliteration	Letter	Latin Transliteration
А а	a	П п	p
Б б	b	Р р	r
В в	v	С с	s
Г г	g	Т т	t
Д д	d	У у	u
Е е	e	Ү ү	ü
Ё ё	ё	Ф ф	f
Ж ж	ž	Х х	x
З з	z	Ц ц	c
И и	i	Ч ч	č
Й й	ï	Ш ш	š
К к	k	Ъ ъ	'
Л л	l	Ы ы	ï
М м	m	Ь ь	'
Н н	n	Э э	è
О о	o	Ю ю	yu
Ө ө	ö	Я я	ya

1.9. Select bibliography

I. LAND AND PEOPLE

Maslennikov, V.A., Contemporary Mongolia, Mongolia Society Publications, Bloomington, Indiana, 1964. (Trans. from the Russian.)

Murzaev, E.M., Die mongolische Volksrepublik, Berlin, 1955. (Trans. from the Russian.)

National Economy of the Mongolian People's Republic for 40 Years, Collection of Statistics, Ulanbator, 1961.

Sanders, A.J.K., The People's Republic of Mongolia, General Reference Guide, London, 1968.

Schurmann, H.F., The Mongols of Afghanistan, An Ethnography of the Moghôls and Related Peoples of Afghanistan, 's-Gravenhage, 1962.

Thiel, E., Die Mongolei: Land, Volk und Wissenschaft der Mongolischen Volksrepublik, München, 1958.

II. HISTORY (including social organization)

Barthold, W., Turkestan Down to the Mongol Invasion, 2nd ed., Oxford, 1928.

Bawden, C.R., The Modern History of Mongolia, London, 1968.

Friters, G.M., Outer Mongolia and its International Position, Baltimore, 1949.

Howorth, H.H., History of the Mongols From the 9th to the 19th Century, Vols. I-IV, London, 1876-1888; Vol. V (Supplements and Indices), London, 1927.

Korostovetz, I.J., Von Cinggis Khan zur Sowjetrepublik. Eine kurze Geschichte der Mongolei unter besonderer Berücksichtigung der neuesten Zeit, Berlin-Leipzig, 1926.

Krader, L., Social Organization of the Mongol-Turkic Pastoral Nomads, The Hague, 1963.

Martin, H.D., The Rise of Chingis Khan and His Conquest of North China, Baltimore, 1950.

Spuler, B., "Die Mongolenzeit", Handbuch der Orientalistik, VI. Band: Geschichte der islamischen Länder, 2ter Abschnitt, Leiden-Köln, 1953.

-----, Die Goldene Horde, Die Mongolen in Russland 1223-1502, Leipzig, 1943.

Vladimircov, B. Ya., The Life of Chingis-Khan, London, 1930. (Trans. from the Russian.)

-----, Le régime sociale des mongols, Le féodalisme nomade, Paris, 1948. (Trans. from the Russian.)

III. CULTURE

Carruthers, Douglas, Unknown Mongolia, Vols. 1-2, London, 1913.

Gilmour, J., Among the Mongols, London, 1888.

Heissig, W., A Lost Civilization, The Mongols Rediscovered, London, 1966. (Trans. from the German.)

Miller, R.J., Monasteries and Culture Change in Inner Mongolia, Wiesbaden, 1959.

Montell, Gösta, "As Ethnographer in China and Mongolia, 1929-1932": S. Hedin, The Sino-Swedish Expedition, Publication No. 26, Stockholm, 1945.

IV. THE MONGOLIAN LANGUAGE

a. Khalkha

Bosson, J.E., Modern Mongolian, A Primer and Reader, Bloomington, Indiana, 1964.

Hangin, J.G., Basic Course in Mongolian, Bloomington, Indiana, 1968.

Luvsandèndèv, A., Mongol'sko-russkiĭ slovar', Pod obščeĭ radakcieĭ, Moskva, 1957.

Poppe, N., Khalkha-Mongolische Grammatik, Mit Bibliographie, Sprachproben und Glossar, Wiesbaden, 1951.

Schalonov Zebek, unter Mitarbeit von Prof. Dr. Johannes Schubert, Mongolisch-Deutsches Wörterbuch, Leipzig, 1961.

Troxel, D.A., Mongolian Vocabulary (Modern Khalkha Language), Mongolian-English, English-Mongolian (Department of the Army Technical Manual TM 30-537), Washington, D.C., 1953.

b. Dariganga

Róna-Tas, A., "A Study of the Dariganga Phonology", Acta Orientalia Hungarica 10:1 (1960), pp. 1-29.

-----, "Dariganga Folklore Texts", ibid., 10:2 (1960), pp. 171-183.

-----, "Dariganga Vocabulary", ibid., 13:1-2 (1961), pp. 147-174.

c. Chakhar

Hattori, S., "Phonemic Structure of Mongol (Chakhar Dialect)", Journal of the Linguistic Society of Japan 19-20 (1951), pp. 68-102.

Jagchid, S., and Dien, A.E., Spoken Chahar Mongolian, Inter-University Program for Chinese Language Studies, n.p. and n.d.

d. Urat

No special works on this dialect are available.

e. Kharchin-Tumut

Nomura, M., "On Short Vowels in the Wang-fu Dialect of the Kharachin Right Banner, Inner Mongolia", Annual Report of the Institute of Ethnology 3 (1940-41).

-----, "Remarks on the Diphthong [wa] in the Kharachin Dialect of the Mongol Language", Journal of the Linguistic Society of Japan 16 (1950), pp. 126-142.

-----, "On Some Phonological Developments in the Kharachin Dialect", Studia Altaica, Wiesbaden, 1957, pp. 132-136.

f. Khorchin

Bosson, J., and Unensecen, B., "Some Notes on the Dialect of the Khorchin Mongols", American Studies in Altaic Linguistics, Bloomington, Indiana, 1962, pp. 23-44.

g. Üjümüchin

Kara, G., "Sur le dialecte üjümücin", Acta Orientalia Hungarica 14:2 (1962), pp. 145-172.

-----, "Un glossaire üjümücin", ibid., 16:1 (1963), pp. 1-43.

h. Ordos

Mostaert, A., "Le dialecte des mongols Urdus (Sud)",
Anthropos 21-22 (1926-27).

-----, Textes oraux ordos, Peip'ing, 1937. (Contains a grammar, pp. xvii-lxx.)

-----, Folklore ordos (Traduction des textes oraux ordos),
Peip'ing, 1947.

-----, Dictionnaire ordos, New York & London, 1968. (Reprint
of the original publication, Peking, 1941-1944.)

Street, J.C., "Urdus Phonology: A Restatement", Ural-Altaische
Jahrbücher 38 (1966), pp. 92-111.

V. OTHER MONGOLIAN LANGUAGES

a. Buriat

Bosson, J.E., Buriat Reader, Bloomington, Indiana, 1963.

Čeremisov, K.M., Buryat-mongol'sko-russkiĭ slovar', Moskva,
1954.

Poppe, N., Buriat Grammar, Bloomington, Indiana, 1960.

b. Oirat

Kara, G., "Notes sur les dialectes oïrat de la Mongolie
Occidentale", Acta Orientalia Hungarica 8:2 (1959),
pp. 111-168.

Todaeva, B.X., "Materialï po fol'kloru sin'czyanskix mongolov",
Tyurko-Mongol'skoe yazïkoznanie i fol'kloristika, Moskva,
1960, pp. 228-264.

Vladimircov, B. Ya., Obrazcï mongol'skoĭ narodnoĭ slovesnosti
(S-Z. Mongoliya), Leningrad, 1926.

c. Kalmyk

Badmaev, B.B., Grammatika kalmïckogo yazïka, Morfologiya,
Èlista, 1966. (In the official Cyrillic alphabet.)

Kotvič, Vl., Opït grammatiki kalmïckogo razgovornogo yazïka,
Izd. II, Rževnice u Pragi, 1929. (Uses a phonetic transcription based on the Russian alphabet.)

Očirov, U.U., Grammatika kalmïckogo yazïka, Sintaksis,
Èlista, 1964. (In the official Cyrillic alphabet.)

Pavlov, D.A., Sostav i klassifikaciya fonem kalmïckogo yazïka, Èlista, 1963.

Ramstedt, G.J., Kalmückisches Wörterbuch, Helsinki, 1935. (Contains a concise grammar; uses a phonetic transcription.)

Russko-Kalmïckiǐ Slovar', pod redakcieǐ I.K. Iliškina, Moskva, 1964. (Uses the official Cyrillic alphabet.)

Street, J.C., "Kalmyk Shwa", American Studies in Altaic Linguistics, Bloomington, Indiana, 1962, pp. 263-291.

d. Moghol

Pritsak, O., "Das Mogholische", Handbuch der Orientalistik, V. Band, Altaistik, Zweiter Abschnitt: Mongolistik, Leiden-Köln, 1964, pp. 159-184.

Ramstedt, G.J., "Mogholica, Beiträge zur Kenntnis der Moghol-Sprache in Afghanistan", Journal de la Société Finno-Ougrienne 23:4 (1905), pp. 1-60.

e. Dagur

Martin, S.E., Dagur Mongolian Grammar, Texts, and Lexicon, Based on the Speech of Peter Onon, Bloomington, Indiana, 1961.

Poppe, N.N., Dagurskoe narečie, Leningrad, 1930.

-----, Über die Sprache der Daguren", Asia Major 10 (1934), pp. 1-32, 183-220.

f. Monguor

de Smedt, A., and Mostaert, A., "Le dialecte monguor parlé par les mongols du Kansou occidental, Ière partie, Phonétique", Anthropos 24-25 (1929-1930).

-----, Le dialecte Monguor parlé par les mongols du Kansou occidental, IIe partie, Grammaire, The Hague-London-Paris, 1964.

-----, Le dialecte Monguor parlé par les mongols du Kansou occidental, IIIe partie, Dictionnaire monguor-français, Peip'ing, 1933.

g. Santa

Todaeva, B.X., Dunsyanskiǐ yazïk, Moskva, 1961.

h. Paongan

Todaeva, B.X., Baoan'skiĭ yazïk, Moskva, 1964.

i. Yellow Uighur

Kotwicz, Wł., "La langue mongole parleé par les Ouïgours Jaunes près de Kan-tcheou", Rocznik Orientalistyczny, Vol. XVI (1953), pp. 435-465.

Mannerheim, C.G.E., "A Visit to the Sarö and Shera Yögurs", Journal de la Société Finno-Ougrienne 27:2 (1911), pp. 1-72.

VI. SCRIPT MONGOLIAN

Haltod, M.; Hangin, J.G.; Kassatkin, S.; and Lessing, F.D., Mongolian-English Dictionary, Berkeley and Los Angeles, 1960.

Poppe, N., Grammar of Written Mongolian, Wiesbaden, 1954; 2nd ed., 1964.

VII. OIRAT SCRIPT LANGUAGE

Popov, A., Grammatika kalmïckago yazïka, Kazan', 1851. (Grammar of the written language of the Kalmyk, which was Script Oirat at that time.)

Pozdněev, A., Kalmïcko-russkiĭ slovar', St. Petersburg, 1911.

Zwick, H.A., Handbuch der westmongolischen Sprache, Donaueschingen, 1853.

VIII. MIDDLE MONGOLIAN

Doerfer, G., "Beiträge zur Syntax der Sprache der Geheimen Geschichte der Mongolen", Central Asiatic Journal 1:4 (1955), pp. 219-267.

Haenisch, E., "Grammatische Besonderheiten in der Sprache der Manghol un Niuca Tobca'an", Studia Orientalia ed. Soc. Orient. Fen. 14:3, pp. 1-26.

Lewicki, M., La langue mongole des transcriptions chinoises du XIVe siècle, Le Houa-yi yi-yu de 1389, Wrocław, 1949; II, Vocabulaire-index, Wrocław, 1959.

Ligeti, L., "Un vocabulaire mongol d'Istanboul", Acta Orientalia Hungarica 14:1 (1962), pp. 3-99.

-----, "Notes sur le vocabulaire mongol d'Istanboul", ibid., 16:2 (1963), pp. 107-174.

Poppe, N., The Mongolian Monuments in ḥP'ags-pa Script, 2nd ed., trans. and ed. by John R. Krueger, Wiesbaden, 1957.

-----, "Das mongolische Sprachmaterial einer Leidener Handschrift", Bulletin de l'Académie des Sciences de l'URSS 1927, pp. 1009-1040, 1251-1274; ibid., 1928, pp. 55-80.

-----, "Das Mittelmongolische", Handbuch der Orientalistik, V. Band, Zweiter Abschnitt: Mongolistik, Leiden-Köln, 1964, pp. 96-103.

Street, J.C., The Language of the Secret History of the Mongols, New Haven, 1957.

IX. COMPARATIVE STUDY OF THE MONGOLIAN LANGUAGES

Poppe, N., Introduction to Mongolian Comparative Studies, Helsinki, 1955.

X. ALTAIC LANGUAGES

Menges, K.H., The Turkic Languages and Peoples, An Introduction to Turkic Studies, Wiesbaden, 1968.

Poppe, N., Introduction to Altaic Linguistics, Wiesbaden, 1965.

Sinor, D., Introduction à l'étude de l'Eurasie Centrale, Wiesbaden, 1963. (A good bibliography.)

2. PHONOLOGY

2.1. The phonemes

Mongolian has the following phonemes: /ə i ɯ u e ө o a p t k b
d g c č ʒ ǰ f s š x w y m n ŋ l r/.

2.11. The consonants

The Mongolian consonant phonemes are shown in Table 8.

Table 8

The consonant phonemes of Mongolian

		Labial	Dental	Velar
Stops	Tense	(/p/)	/t/	(/k/)
	Lax	/b/	/d/	/g/
Affricates	Tense		/c/ /č/	
	Lax		/ʒ/ /ǰ/	
Fricatives	Tense	(/f/)	/s/ /š/	/x/
	Lax	(/w/)	/y/	
Nasals		/m/	/n/	/ŋ/
Liquids			/l/	
			/r/	

Note: Phonemes which are alien to Mongolian and occur only in
loan words are enclosed in parentheses.

2.111. The tense stops

The tense stops /p t k/ are voiceless and with the exception of
/t/, are aspirated in all positions.

    (1) /p/ is a tense voiceless bilabial stop and resembles

English p in pin. It occurs only in loan words. Most speakers do not distinguish between /p/ and /f/.

/puɯʐə/ [pʰɯ̄ʐě] 'shop'

/sampiŋ/ [sȧmpʰɪ̆~] 'abacus'

(2) /t/ is a tense voiceless apico-dental or post-dental stop. It is acoustically similar to English t in ten. There are two allophones: [tʰ], which is aspirated, and [t], which is unaspirated. Of these, [t] occurs initially when the second syllable is short and has a tense consonant at its onset.

/too/ [tʰɔ̄] 'number'

/utaa/ [u̯tʰā] 'smoke'

/tatəxə/ [tatʰăχ̆ă] 'to pull'

/urtə/ [u̯Rtʰă] 'long'

(3) /k/ is a tense voiceless dorso-velar aspirated stop. It occurs only in recent loan words, and most speakers substitute /x/ for it.

/kapitaal/ [kʰapʰitʰāɫ] 'capital'

2.112. The lax stops

The lax stops /b d g/, with the exception of /d/, which is always voiceless, have voiced and voiceless allophones.

(1) /b/ is a lax bilabial stop. Its allophones are [b w B W]. The allophone [b] is a voiced bilabial stop identical with English b in bear. It occurs only in medial position, after /m/ and /l/, and before a vowel.

/umbəxə/ [u̯mbăχ̆ă] 'to wade, to walk in water'

/elbəg/ [elběG] 'plentiful'

The allophone [w] is a voiced bilabial fricative. It is important to note that it is not a semivowel and is very different from English w. It is comparable to Spanish b [β] in Habana. This allophone occurs intervocalically, after /r/ in medial position, in syllable-final position before a lax consonant, and in final position in monosyllabic words.

/yabə/ [yȧwă] 'go!'

/arbə/ [arwă] 'ten'

/yabgəŋ/ [yåwgă~] 'pedestrian'

/ab/ [aw] 'take!'

The allophone [B] is a lax voiceless bilabial stop (<u>media lenis</u>). It resembles acoustically initial <u>b</u> in some German dialects and gives the impression of a consonant intermediate between <u>b</u> and unaspirated <u>p</u>. It occurs initially, in word-final position in polysyllabic words, and in syllable-final position before a tense consonant.

/bar/ [Bar] 'tiger'

/teləb/ [tʰellə̆B] 'appearance'

/abtəx/ [aBtʰăχă] 'to be taken'

The allophone [W] is a voiceless bilabial fricative, the voiceless counterpart of [w]. It occurs in syllable-final position before a tense consonant. In word-final position, it occurs in words of two or more syllables.

/absəŋ/ [aWsă~] 'one who has taken'

/teləb/ [tʰellə̆W] 'appearance'

(2) /g/ is a lax dorso-velar consonant. Some allophones are deep-velar (back-velar), other allophones are front-velar. Some allophones are stops, other are fricatives. The allophones are [G̣ g̣ ɣ G g g̣]. The allophones [G g g̣] occur only with front vowels; the allophones [G̣ g̣ ɣ] occur only with back vowels. The allophones [G̣ g̣ G g] are stops; the allophones [ɣ g̣] are fricatives. The allophones [G̣ G] are voiceless; the allophones [g̣ ɣ g g̣] are voiced.

The allophone [G̣] is a lax voiceless back-velar stop. It occurs in words with back vowels in initial position, in word-final position, and in syllable-final position before tense consonants.

/gar/ [G̣ar] 'hand'

/agtə/ [aG̣tʰă] 'gelding'

/ug/ [uG̣] 'foundation, primary'

The allophone [g] is a lax voiced back-velar stop. It occurs in medial position after /b m ŋ l r/ in words with back vowels.

/yabgəŋ/ [yåwgă~] 'on foot, pedestrian'

/amgae/ [amgáė] 'the bit of the bridle'

/uŋgəldəxə/ [uŋgăɬDăχă] 'to neigh'

/gargəxə/ [Gargăχă] 'to take out'

The allophone [ɣ] is a back-velar voiced fricative. It occurs only in intervocalic position in words with back vowels.

/bagə/ [Baɣă] 'small'

/unəgaaxə/ [unăɣāχă] 'to drop, to make fall down'

The allophone [G] is a lax voiceless front-velar stop. It occurs only in words with front vowels and in the same positions as [G̱], i.e. initially, in word-final position, and before tense consonants in medial position.

/ger/ [Ger] 'yurt'

/egcə/ [eGcʰĕ] 'steep'

/əg/ [əG] 'give!'

The allophone [g] is identical with English g in gate. It is a lax voiced front-velar stop. It occurs in words with front vowels in medial position after /m ŋ l r/ and before a vowel. It occurs also intervocalically, in which position it often alternates with [g̱].

/emgəŋ/ [emgĕ~] 'old woman'

/əŋgərxə/ [əŋgŏrxŏ] 'to pass'

/ergə/ [ergĕ] 'steep bank'

/degee/ [Degē͡] or [Deg̱ē͡] 'hook'

The allophone [g̱] is a lax voiced front-velar fricative. It occurs only in intervocalic position in words with front vowels, alternating with [g].

/degee/ [Degē͡] or Deg̱ē͡] 'hook'

(3) /d/ is a lax voiceless apico-dental stop (media lenis) which has only one allophone, namely [D]. In medial position, between a single vowel phoneme and shwa, it is usually geminate, i.e. [DD].

/darxə/ [Darχă] 'to press'

/dotər/ [Dɔtʰŏr] 'inside, within'

32

/adxə/ [aDχǎ] 'handful'

/ed/ [eD] 'goods, material'

/modə/ [mɔDDǒ] 'tree'

/modoor/ [mɔDɔ̄r] 'by means of a tree'

2.113. The tense affricates

The tense affricates are /c č/. A phonemic distinction between these two affricates exists in Khalkha, Kharchin, and some other dialects, but does not exist in Chakhar, Urat, Ordos, and Khorchin. Examples: Khalkha /cadəxə/ 'to be satiated' and /čadəxə/ 'to be able', but Chakhar /čadəxə/ 'to be satiated' and /čádəxə/ 'to be able'.

(1) /c/ is a tense dental or post-dental affricate which resembles English [ts] in that's it. It has two allophones: [cʰ], which is aspirated and [c], which is not aspirated.

The allophone [c] occurs initially when the following short syllable begins with a tense consonant.

/casəŋ/ [cassǎ~] 'made of snow'

/cacəg/ [cacʰäG] 'fringe'

The allophone [cʰ] is a tense dental or post-dental aspirated affricate. It occurs initially and medially.

/cagaan/ [cʰaɣā~] 'white'

/acrəxə/ [acʰrǎχǎ] 'to bring'

/acə/ [acʰǎ] 'fork, pitchfork'

(2) /č/ is a tense alveolar or post-alveolar affricate comparable to English ch. It has the allophones [č] and [čʰ].

The allophone [č] is unaspirated and occurs in initial position when the second syllable begins with a tense consonant and the vowel of the second syllable is a shwa.

/čuxəl/ [ču̧χχǎɬ] 'important'

The allophone [čʰ] is aspirated. It occurs initially and medially.

/čuluu/ [čʰu̧ɬū̧] 'stone'

/čarae/ [čʰárạ̈ẹ] 'face'

/či/ [čʰi] 'thou'

2.114. The lax affricates

The lax affricates are /ʒ/ and /ǰ/. No phonemic distinction
exists between them in Ordos, Chakhar, Urat, and Khorchin.

(1) /ʒ/ is a lax voiceless dental or post-dental affricate, comparable to English dz in adze. In intervocalic position, between a single vowel phoneme and shwa, it is usually
geminate, i.e. [ʒʒ].

/garʒə/ [Ga̧rǯǎ] 'financial loss'

/ʒaxə/ [ʒaχχǎ] 'edge, border'

/gaʒər/ [Ga̧ʒʒǎr] 'country, land'

(2) /ǰ/ is a lax voiceless alveolar or post-alveolar affricate. It is acoustically close to English j. Intervocalically, between a single vowel and /i/, it is usually geminate.

/ǰil/ [ǰil] 'year'

/ɵnǰixə/ [ɵnǰǐxɵ̆] 'to spend two nights and a day between
them'

/aǰig/ [a̧ǰǰɪ̇G] 'attention'

2.115. The fricatives

Mongolian has six fricatives, namely /f w s š y x/. Of them,
/f w/ are bilabial; /š y/ are fronto-alveolar; /s/ is dental or
post-dental; and /x/ is dorso-velar.

(1) /f/ is a tense bilabial fricative similar to English
f. It occurs only in recent loan words. Most Mongols do not
distinguish between /p/ and /f/, and use them indiscriminately.
The phonetic value of /f/ is [φ].

/faabrig/ [φābrɪ̇G] 'plant, factory'

(2) /w/ is a lax bilabial fricative. In genuine Mongolian words [w] occurs only as an allophone of /b/ (see
2.112.), but in loan words [w] occurs in positions in which
the [w] allophone of /b/ does not occur.

/waar/ [wār] 'tile' < Chinese

/wiiʒə/ [wīʒǎ] 'visa' < Russian < Western languages

(3) /s/ is a tense voiceless dental or post-dental fricative identical with English s in song. It is usually geminate

34

between a single vowel phoneme in the initial syllable and a shwa in the second syllable.

/sar/ [sar] 'moon, month'

/bəs/ [Bəs] 'cotton cloth'

/asuuxə/ [asū̜χă] 'to ask'

/usəndə/ [u̜ssănDă] 'in water'

/tasəlχə/ [tassăɨχă] 'to tear apart'

(4) /š/ is a tense voiceless fronto-alveolar fricative identical with English sh. Between a single vowel phoneme of the initial syllable and /i/ of the second syllable, it is usually geminate.

/šar/ [šar] 'yellow'

/aašilxə/ [āšĭ̄ɨχă] 'to be angry'

/xašaa/ [χašā] 'fence, court'

/tašixə/ [taššĭχă] 'to hit, to strike'

(5) /y/ is a lax fronto-alveolar fricative comparable to English y. It has little or no friction in word-initial position, but in medial position, between vowels, and in final position the friction is rather strong. Between a single vowel of the initial syllable and a shwa of the following syllable, /y/ is usually geminate.

/yabəxə/ [yåwăχă] 'to go'

/xayaad/ [χayāD] 'having thrown'

/xayəxə/ [χayyăχă] 'to throw'

/ayə/ [ayyă] 'circumstance'

/abyaa/ [awyā] 'let us take!'

(6) /x/ is a tense voiceless dorso-velar fricative which is acoustically close to Gaelic ch in loch. It has the allophones [x ^{k}x χ ^{k}χ], all of which are usually geminate between the single vowel of the initial syllable and the shwa of the second syllable.

The allophone [x] is a tense fronted dorso-velar fricative and occurs initially in words with front vowels, and medially before a geminate vowel or diphthong.

/xeŋ/ [xeŋ] 'who'

/xəxee/ [xöxə̄] 'cuckoo'

/exə/ [exxə̆] 'mother'

The allophone [ᵏx] is an affricate which begins as a stop and ends as a fricative. It occurs in words with front vowels instead of [x] in some dialects, but in almost all dialects after a consonant in medial position.

/eŋxə/ [eŋ̇ᵏxə̆] 'peace'

The allophone [χ] is a tense voiceless back-velar (deep-velar) fricative. It occurs only with back vowels in initial position and after a consonant in medial position.

/xarə/ [χarə̆] 'black'

/uxaa/ [u̯χā] 'hill'

/axə/ [aχχə̆] 'elder brother, elder, uncle'

The allophone [ᵏ̣χ] is a back-velar tense affricate which begins as [ḳ] and ends as [χ]. It occurs in back-vocalic words in positions in which front-vocalic words have [ᵏχ].

/aŋxə/ [aŋ̇ᵏ̣χə̆] 'beginning'

/xatuu/ [ᵏ̣χatʰū̱] 'difficult'

2.116. <u>The nasals</u>

The nasals are /m n ŋ/.

(1) /m/ is a bilabial nasal identical with English <u>m</u>. It has only one allophone, which is [m].

/mal/ [mał] 'cattle'

/em/ [em] 'medicine'

(2) /n/ is an apico-dental or post-dental nasal identical with English <u>n</u>. It has only one allophone, which is [n]. Between the single vowel of the initial syllable and the shwa of the second syllable, it is usually geminate.

/nar/ [nar] 'sun'

/endə/ [eṅDə̆] 'here'

/enə/ [eṅnə̆] 'this'

(3) /ŋ/ is a dorso-velar nasal similar to English <u>ng</u> in <u>song</u>. It has two main allophones, [ŋ] and [˜].

36

The allophone [ŋ] is a dorso-velar nasal with complete
oral closure. It occurs medially before /g x k/, and at the
end of monosyllabic words with short vowels. (If we take into
consideration that in words with back vowels, [ŋ] becomes back-
velar, the allophone [ŋ] actually becomes two allophones, [ŋ]
and [ŋ̬].)

/aŋxə/ [aŋᵏχǎ] 'beginning'
/eŋxə/ [ėŋᵏxě] 'peace'
/oŋ/ [ɔŋ] 'year'

The allophone [~] is nasalization of the vowel, or, more
precisely, the nasalized end of a vowel. It is rather weak and
is the result of incomplete oral closure. It occurs finally in
monosyllabic words, the vowel of which is geminate or a diphthong. It also occurs at the end of words of two or more syllables.

/xaaŋ/ [χā~] 'khan, king'
/ulaaŋ/ [u̯lā~] 'red'
/čineeŋ/ [čʰinē~] 'the size of'
/aŋxəŋ/ [aŋᵏxa~] 'initial'

2.117. The liquids

Mongolian has a lax apico-dental or post-dental phoneme /l/ and
the apical trill /r/.

(1) /l/ has a decrescendo voicing before a tense consonant
or in word-final position. It is dark when preceded and/or
followed by back vowels. In words with front vowels, and before
/i/ in all words, it is light and corresponds to French or German
l in lèvre or leben, respectively. When final /i/ disappears,
e.g. in fast speech, its trace is the palatalization of /l/,
i.e. the allophone is [lʲ]. Consequently, the allophones are
[L l lʲ ɫ ᶅ]. Intervocalically, between the single vowel phoneme of the initial syllable and the shwa of the following syllable, /l/ is often geminate, i.e. [ll] or [ɫɫ].

The allophone [l] occurs in words with front vowels, and
before /i/ in words with back vowels. It is comparable to

37

French or German <u>l</u>.

/bel/ [Bel] 'waist'

/elbəg/ [elbĕG] 'plentiful'

/eləs/ [ellĕs] 'sand'

/luɯɯ/ [lū̅] 'basket'

The allophone [L] occurs in medial position before tense consonants in words with front vowels. It is comparable to English <u>l</u> in <u>full</u>.

/xeltəgii/ [xeLtʰĕgī̆] 'oblique'

The allophone [ɫ] is a dark lax apico-dental phoneme which resembles Russian л in палка. It occurs in words with back vowels.

/aləxə/ [aɫɫăχă] 'to kill'

/lamə/ [ɫamă] 'Buddhist priest'

/xaalgə/ [χāɫgă] 'gate'

/galuu/ [Gaɫū̲] 'goose'

The allophone [Ł] is the voiceless counterpart of [ɫ]. It occurs before tense consonants in words with back vowels.

/altə/ [aŁtʰă] 'gold'

The allophone [lʲ] appears where /i/ has disappeared. The palatalization is the trace of that /i/.

/surguuli/ [surgū̲lï̆] or [surgū̲lʲ] 'school'

Note: The only phonemically geminate consonant is /ll/, e.g. /emeelee/ 'his own saddle (accus.)', /emeellee/ 'please saddle!'.

(2) /r/ is an apical trill. Before a tense consonant it is decrescendo voiced and often becomes completely unvoiced, like Russian р in Петр. This allophone is [R]. The other allophone, [r], occurs in all the other positions. There are no genuine Mongolian words with /r/ at the onset. Most speakers cannot pronounce an initial /r/, and prefix a prosthetic vowel.

/ger/ [Ger] 'yurt'

/irsəŋ/ [irsĕ~] 'one who has come'

/urtə/ [uRtʰă] 'long'

/oryooŋ/ [ɔryɔ̃~] 'district' < Russian < French <u>rayon</u>

/araadi/ [arāDɪ̆] 'radio' < Russian < Western

languages

2.12. The vowels

The vowels occur (1) as single vowel phonemes, e.g. /a/; (2) as geminate vowel phonemes, e.g. /aa/; (3) as diphthongs, e.g. /ae/.

In most of the dialects there are seven strong or fully articulated vowel phonemes /e ə ɯ i a o u/ and one weak or over-short vowel phoneme /ə/, which can be characterized as shwa. The vowel phonemes are shown in Table 9.

Table 9

The vowel phonemes of Mongolian

| | | Unrounded | Rounded | |
			Front	Back
Strong	High	/i/	/ɯ/	/u/
	Mid	/e/	/ə/	/o/
	Low	/a/		
Weak		/ə/		

Single strong (fully articulated) vowel phonemes, with the exception of /i/, occur in most of the dialects only in the initial syllable (Ordos seems to be the only dialect in which single strong vowel phonemes occur in all syllables). The strong vowel phonemes occur, however, as geminates or as components of diphthongs, in all syllables in all dialects.

The weak (overshort) vowel phoneme occurs only in non-initial syllables. (Ordos does not have this phoneme.)

2.121. The phoneme /e/

The phoneme /e/ is the class of mid-front vowels. Its allophones are [e ē ė ę̇ ę ε̄].

The allophone [e] is a mid-front unrounded vowel, more or
less like English e in den. It occurs in monosyllabic words
and in polysyllabic words with /ə/ or /ee/ in the second syllable, and also as the second component of the diphthongs /ae
oe/ in non-initial syllables. It occurs after any consonant
but the velars and /y/. Geminate /ee/ occurs in all positions,
as [ē].

    /em/ [em] 'medicine'
    /ertə/ [eRtʰě] 'early'
    /xeer/ [xēr] 'steppe, desert'
    /erees/ [erēs] 'screw'
    /dalae/ [Daɫǎe] 'sea'
    /noxoe/ [nɔχǒe] 'dog'

The allophone [ė] is a mid-high front unrounded vowel which
sounds like something between English e in pen and i in pin.
It occurs in the initial syllable when followed by /č ǰ š/; in
words with /i/ in the second syllable; and after /y/.

    /ečixə/ [ėčʰǐxě] 'to go away'
    /xešig/ [xėššǐG] 'bliss'
    /yendər/ [yenDěr] 'platform, tribune'

The allophone [ę̇] is nonsyllabic [ė]. It occurs as the
second component of the diphthongs /ae oe/ in the initial syllable or in monosyllabic words.

    /aexə/ [äę̇χǎ] 'to be afraid'
    /oe/ [oę̇] 'forest, grove'

The allophone [ę] is a centralized unrounded vowel. It is
articulated with the tongue retracted and is described as a mid-
high central open vowel. It occurs after velar consonants in
the initial syllable.

    /xeŋ/ [xęŋ] 'who'
    /gedəs/ [GęDDěs] 'intestines'

The allophone [ɛ̄] occurs only as a long vowel in noninitial syllables in emphatic speech, where is replaces [ē] = /ee/.

/tertee/ [tertʰɛ̄] 'on the farther side (don't you see it?)'

2.122. The phoneme /ə/

The phoneme /ə/ is the class of rounded mid or low front or fronted-central vowels. Its allophones are [ö ɔ̄ ə].

The allophone [ö] occurs in the initial syllable when the next vowel is /ee/. It is identical with German ö̲ or French e̲u̲.

/gərees/ [Görɔ̄s] 'antelope'

The allophone [ɔ̄] is phonemically /ee/. It is a low fronted-central rounded vowel somewhat resembling Swedish ö̲ in fö̲r.

/eəree/ [ɔ̄rɔ̄] 'himself'

The allophone [ə] occurs in all other positions. It is a mid-high fronted-central rounded vowel which somewhat resembles Southern Swedish u̲ in lund.

/xəl/ [xəl] 'foot'
/ədər/ [əDDə̆r] 'day'

2.123. The phoneme /ɯ/

The phoneme /ɯ/ is the class of rounded high-front or central vowels. Its allophones are [ü ü̆ ɯ ɯ̄].

The allophone [ü] is a high-front rounded vowel, identical with German ü̲ and French u̲. It occurs as the first component of the diphthong /ɯi/ in the initial syllable, and after /y/ in the initial syllable.

/gɯi/ [Güi̭] 'run!'
/yɯldə/ [yülDə̆] 'herpes'

The allophone [ü̆] is a very short [ü], a glide which occurs as the first component of the diphthong /ɯi/ in noninitial syllables.

/ədɯi/ [əDü̆i] 'not yet'

The allophone [ɯ] is a rounded fronted-central high vowel
which resembles Norwegian u in hus. It occurs in the initial
syllable in all the other positions. Geminate /ɯɯ/ is [ɯ̄]; it
occurs in all syllables.

/bɯs/ [Bɯs] 'belt'

/sɯɯ/ [sɯ̄] 'milk'

/xelɯɯlxə/ [xe̦lɯ̄lxə̆] 'to let say'

2.124.   The phoneme /i/

The phoneme /i/ is the class of high front or central unrounded
vowels. It has the allophones [i ī̦ ĭ ⁱ i̧].

The allophone [i] is a high front unrounded vowel, more or
less like English i in shin. It occurs in the initial syllable.

/irə/ [irə̆/ 'come!'

/bičig/ [Bičʰ ĬG] 'letter'

The allophone [ī̦] is phonemically the geminate /ii/ in
initial position or after /t b d g c ʒ s x m n l r/. It is a
fronted-central high unround vowel.

/iimə/ [ī̦mə̆] 'such'

/xii/ [xī̦] 'air'

/tiimə/ [tʰī̦mə̆] 'such as that'

The allophone [ĭ] occurs only in noninitial syllables.
It is a short [i].

/ami/ [amĭ] 'life'

/barixə/ [Barĭxă] 'to catch'

The allophone [ⁱ] is an overshort [i], a glide before other
vowels. It is the nonsyllabic element of the diphthongs /ia io/
in the initial syllable, and /iaa ioo iuu/ in the noninitial
syllables.

/nialxə/ [nⁱäɫxă] 'infant'

/aliaa/ [aɫⁱā] 'naughty, frolicsome'

/xoliood/ [xoɫⁱōD] 'having mixed'

The allophone [i̧] is the nonsyllabic element of the diphthongs /ui ɯi/.

/uiləxə/ [ui̯ɫäχä] 'to weep'

/ʒѡil/ [ʒüi̯l] 'kind, sort'

2.125. The phoneme /a/

The phoneme /a/ is the class of low unrounded vowels which includes front, central, and back vowels. Its allophones are
[ä á ǎ a ā], and in some dialects [å].

The allophone [ä] is a low front unrounded vowel that resembles English a in bat. It occurs in the diphthongs /ia/ and
/ae/ in the initial syllable or in monosyllabic words.

/nialxə/ [nⁱä̈ɫχä] 'infant'

/saeŋ/ [säę̈~] or [säę̈ŋ] 'good'

/aexə/ [ä̈ę̈χä] 'to be afraid'

The allophone [á] is an unrounded low central vowel, close
to French a in madame. It occurs in the initial syllable before
a syllable with /i/.

/ami/ [ámǐ] 'life'

/aliaa/ [ál ⁱā] 'naughty, frolicsome'

The allophone [ǎ] is a short [á] and occurs as the first
component of the diphthong /ae/ in noninitial syllables.

/dalae/ [Daɫǎe] 'sea'

The allophone [å] is a slightly rounded [a]. It occurs
only before /b/ in some dialects in the western part of the
Mongolian People's Republic.

/yabəxə/ [yåwǎχä] 'to go, to walk'

The allophone [a] is the "pure" Italian a in padre. It
occurs in all the other positions.

/amə/ [amǎ] 'mouth'

/xarə/ [χarǎ] 'black'

The allophone [ā] is geminate /aa/ in all positions.

/xaalgə/ [χāɫgǎ] 'gate'

/ulaaŋ/ [uɫā~] 'red'

2.126. The phoneme /o/

The phoneme /o/ is the class of lower-mid rounded back or central vowels. Its allophones are [ɔ ō o ō ŏ].

The allophone [ɔ] is an open, low-mid rounded back vowel close to English aw in saw. It occurs in the initial syllable, before /ə/ in the following syllable, and in monosyllabic words. Geminate /oo/ occurs as [ō] in these positions.

/oŋ/ [ɔŋ] 'year'

/modə/ [mɔDDŏ] 'tree'

/oosər/ [ōsər] 'tape'

The allophone [o] is the French o in homme. It occurs in the diphthong /oe/ in the initial syllable, after /i/ or /y/, and before /i/ of the second syllable. Geminate /oo/ occurs as [ō] in these positions.

/xoenə/ [Xoėnŏ] 'afterwards'

/niombə/ [nⁱombŏ] 'meditation' < Tibetan

/yorə/ [yorŏ] 'omen'

/mori/ [morĭ] 'horse'

/moriooroo/ [morĭōrŏ] 'by his own horse'

The allophone [ŏ] is a short [o] and occurs as a component of the diphthong /oe/ in noninitial syllables.

/noxoe/ [nɔXŏe] 'dog'

2.127. The phoneme /u/

The phoneme /u/ is the class of high back rounded vowels. Its allophones are [u̯ ū̯ u ū ŭ].

The allophone [u̯] is a back vowel produced with the larynx considerably lowered. It gives the acoustic impression of being a vowel between English oo in door and oo in foot. The allophone [u̯] occurs in all positions except before a syllable with /i/, immediately before or after /i/, and immediately after /y/. The allophone [ū̯] is geminate /uu/ and occurs in the same positions.

/us/ [u̯s] 'water'

/ulaaŋ/ [u̯la̅~] 'red'

/uul/ [u̅ɫ] 'original'

The allophone [u] is higher than [u̯] and comes closer to the French ou in ouvert. It occurs before a syllable with /i/ and immediately after /y/. It also forms the first component of the diphthong /ui/ in initial syllables. The allophone [u̅] is geminate /uu/ and occurs in the same positions as [u].

/ulig/ [ullĭG] 'nuisance'

/uliaas/ [uli̅as] 'poplar'

/yum/ [yum] 'something'

/uiləxə/ [ui̯lăχă] 'to weep'

/taniuulxə/ [tʰȧni̯u̅ɫχă] 'to make acquainted'

The allophone [ŭ] is a short [u]. It occurs as the first component of the diphthong /ui/ in noninitial syllables.

/xarəŋxui/ [χarăŋ̍kχŭi] 'darkness'

2.128. The phoneme /ə/

The phoneme /ə/ is the class of weak or overshort mid-front, central, or back vowels. It occurs only in noninitial syllables. Its allophones are [ĕ ă ə̆ ŏ], the selection depending on the vowel of the preceding syllable, unless this vowel is either /ə/ or /i/ in a noninitial syllable, in which case it is conditioned by the vowel preceding /ə/ or /i/. Also, when the vowel of the preceding syllable is one of the diphthongs /ae oe ui ɯi/, the quality of /ə/ is conditioned by the first, rather than the second, member of the diphthong.

The allophone [ĕ] is an overshort, reduced [e], more or less like English a in sofa. It occurs after /e ee i ii ɯ ɯɯ ɯi/ in a preceding syllable.

/enə/ [enĕ] or [ennĕ] 'this'

/deerə/ [De̅rĕ] 'on, above'

/irsəŋ/ [irsĕ~] 'one who has come'

/tiimə/ [tʰi̅mĕ] 'such one'

/ɯnə/ [ɯnĕ] 'price'

/tʉʉndə/ [tʰʉ̄nDĕ] 'to him'

/ɯilə/ [ü̧ilĕ] 'work'

/erxiləgči/ [ėrxǐlĕGčʰ ĭ] 'manager'

The allophone [ă] is an overshort, reduced [a]. It occurs after /a aa ae u uu ui/.

/arbəŋ/ [arwă~] 'ten'

/baatər/ [Bāt ʰăr] 'hero'

/aexəbtər/ [ä̧ẹxăWtʰăr] 'terrible'

/urəŋ/ [u̧ră~] 'skillful'

/uurləxə/ [ūr łăxă] 'to become angry'

/uiləxə/ [u̧i łăxă] 'to weep'

The allophone [ɔ̆] is an overshort, reduced [ɔ]. It occurs after /o oo oe/.

/modə/ [mɔDDɔ̆] 'tree'

/oosər/ [ɔ̄sɔ̆r] 'tape'

/oelgəxə/ [oė łgɔ̆xɔ̆] 'to understand'

/orčimdə/ [ɔrčʰ ĭmDɔ] 'in the vicinity'

The allophone [ĕ] is an overshort, reduced [ə]. It occurs after /ə əə/.

/ədər/ [əDDĕr] 'day'

/bəərə/ [B ɔ̄rĕ] 'kidney'

2.13. Juncture

There are three types of juncture: One internal open juncture /+/; and two terminal junctures, namely, the comma juncture /,/ and the final-pause juncture /./.

The comma juncture is usually accompanied by a rising pitch, but the final-pause juncture is accompanied by a falling pitch.

The compound juncture occurs in words compounded of two independent words. The juncture between them is close, with assimilation of some consonants and with fusion of the vowels, the initial vowel of the second word absorbing the final /ə/ of the first word. The compound has one main stress, which is on the strongest syllable of the compound.

/šaršəbuu/ [šaršăwū́] 'owl', but

/šar+šubuu/ [šáʼr šuwū́] 'yellow bird' (any yellow bird)

/xarxɯŋ/ [χaʼɾxw̃ŋ] 'commoner, layman', but

/xar+xɯŋ/ [χaʼr xɯʼŋ] 'black man'

2.14. Stress

The stress is expiratory and strong. It is predictable; consequently, nonphonemic.

Words containing no geminate vowel phonemes or diphthongs
have the stress on the initial syllable.

/axə/ [aʼχχă] 'elder brother'

/uŋšisəɲ/ [uʼŋšĭsă~] 'having read'

Words containing one geminate vowel phoneme or one diphthong have the stress on the geminate vowel or diphthong,
respectively.

/galuu/ [Ɠaɬū́] 'goose'

/dalae/ [Daɬăe'] 'sea'

Words containing more than one geminate vowel phoneme or
diphthong have the stress on the penultimate geminate vowel or
diphthong.

/moriooroo/ [morⁱṓʼrō̄] 'by means of his own horse'

/dalaegaaraa/ [Daɬăeɣā́ʼrā̄] 'by means of his own sea'

2.15. Emphatic accent

The emphatic accent occurs only on the last vowel of a word.
In polysyllabic words, all preceding vowels have their normal
pitch, but the last vowel receives either a falling or rising
pitch.

/darǰáa./ [Darǰá́.] 'Darja!' (simple emphasis or address)

/darǰáa,/ [Darǰá̌,] 'Darja, indeed?' (surprise)

2.2. Phonotactics

Only the most important information will be supplied here, as
a preliminary to the discussion of the morphophonemics (see 2.3.).

2.21. Vowels and vowel sequences

Table 10, adapted from Street's Khalkha Structure (p. 65), shows
the vowel sequences which occur as phonemic nuclei in the native
vocabulary of the Khalkha dialect.

Table 10

Phonemic nuclei

	10	20	30	40	50	60	70	80	90
	V	iV	Vi/Ve	Vu	VV	iVV	uVV	uVe	Vii
1	a	ia	ae	au	aa	iaa	uaa	uae	
2	o	io	oe		oo	ioo			
3	e				ee				
4	ə				əə				
5	u		ui		uu	iuu			
6	ɯ		ɯi		ɯɯ				
7	i				ii				
8	ə								əii

The occurrences are illustrated below. Note that 11 (the
intersection of column 10 and row 1) is /a/; 36 (the intersection
of column 30 and row 6) is /ɯi/; 54 is /əə/, etc.

> 10 single vowel:
> 11 /tanae/ 'your', 12 /odoo/ 'now', 13 /xeŋ/ 'who',
> 14 /šenə/ 'night', 15 /ulaaŋ/ 'red', 16 /ɯgə/ 'word',
> 17 /bičig/ 'letter', 18 /enə/ 'this'
>
> 20 /i/ and a single vowel:
> 21 /miaŋgə/ 'thousand', 22 /niombə/ 'meditation' <
> Tibetan
>
> 30 single vowel and /i/ or /e/:
> 31 /saeŋ/ 'good', 32 /oe/ 'forest', 35 /uiləxə/ 'to
> weep', 36 /ɯilə/ 'work'
>
> 40 Single vowel and /u/. Occurs only in one word and is
> probably a borrowing from Script Mongolian: 41 /augaa/
> 'might'

50 a geminate vowel phoneme:

51 /xaa/ 'where?', 52 /too/ 'number', 53 /deerees/
'from above', 54 /ɵɵrɵɵ/ 'oneself', 55 /uu/ 'drink!',
56 /suɯ/ 'milk', 57 /tiimə/ 'such'

60 /i/ and a geminate vowel phoneme:

61 /xiaa/ 'aide-de-camp', 62 /xoliood/ 'having mixed',
65 /xariuu/ 'answer'

70 /u/ and a geminate vowel phoneme:

71 /guaa/ 'beauty'

80 /u/ plus vowel plus /e/:

81 /guae/ 'Mr.'

90 single vowel and /ii/:

98 /axəiiŋ/ 'of the elder brother'

2.22. Vowel harmony

The vowels of Mongolian are restricted as far as their occurrence in a word is concerned. The rules restricting their
occurrence are called "vowel harmony". This term implies that
the vowels must "harmonize" or "agree" with each other within
a word. The general rule is that, with the exceptions of
/ə i ii/ in noninitial syllables, either only front vowels
/e ɵ ɯ/ or only back vowels /a o u/ may occur in one word.
This applies to both single and geminate vowel phonemes. The
diphthongs are classified as front or back according to whether
the vowel other than /i/ or /e/ is front or back, e.g. /ɯi/ is
front, but /ui/, /ae/, and /ia/ are back. Table 11 shows the
possible occurrences.

The vowel harmony rules apply to vowels within all morphemes which constitute a word or a word-form. There are only
a few exceptions.

Compound words do not comply with the vowel harmony: each
member of the compound retains its own vowels. These are mostly
names of people, places, etc.: /cerəndulmaa/ 'Tserendulmaa'
(woman's name).

49

Table 11
Vowel harmony

After:	May occur:		
/a aa ae/ or /u uu ui/	/aa ae/	/uu ui/	/i ii/ and /ə/
/o oo oe/	/oo oe/		
/e ee/ or /ɯ ɯɯ ɯi/	/ee/	/ɯɯ ɯi/	
/ө өө/	/өө/		
/i ii/ in an initial syllable	/ee/		
/ə/ in a noninitial syllable	any vowel		

Examples: /xaanaasaa/ 'where from?', /yabaarae/ 'go
(later)!', /xatuu/ 'hard', /xarəŋxui/ 'darkness', /utaa/
'smoke', /untuu/ 'anger', /burgui/ 'needle for cleaning
the pipe', /xodoodə/ 'colon (intestine)', /oruulxə/ 'to
put in', /bolxuicə/ 'as far as possible', /erees/ 'screw',
/xelɯɯlxə/ 'to let say', /bɯrɯi/ 'dusk', /egөөmər/ 'gener-
ous', /өөрөө/ 'oneself', /өdɯi/ 'not yet', /bөөрəŋxɯi/
'round, spherical', /irəxə/ 'to come', /iimə/ 'such',
/xiigeer/ 'by means of air', /irɯɯleed/ 'having made come'.

Foreign names and recent borrowings from other languages
also retain their original vowels: /germaani/ 'Germany',
/pioneer/ 'pioneer' (Boy Scouts).

50

A few suffix morphemes do not comply with the harmony:
/oegɯi/ 'treeless, bare of forests', /yabəǰee/ 'he went',
/ərtee/ 'indebted', etc.

2.23. Occurrence of consonants

Not all consonants occur in all positions, and the general rule
is that consonant clusters do not occur initially.

2.231. Single consonants

The phoneme /ŋ/ does not occur in syllable- or word-initial
position. All other consonants may occur in syllable-initial
and, with the exception of /r/, in word-initial position.
There are only a few native words with initial /l/.

Initial /r/ does not occur in native words. Loanwords with
initial /r/ receive a prosthetic vowel, e.g. /araadi/ 'radio' <
Russian < Western languages.

The tense stops, the affricates /c ʒ č ǰ/, and the velar
fricative /x/ do not occur in syllable- or word-final position.

2.232. Two consonants

Not all consonants form clusters with all other consonants.
For example, in normal speech, such clusters as /bm bn dc dʒ
dǰ ds dn/ do not occur. In fast speech, elision of /ə/ may
occur, and in such a case a cluster may appear which is alien
to normal speech and which is not supported by the facts of
Mongolian grammar, e.g. [ɯʒtʰĕl] 'while he was looking' is
phonemically /ɯʒətəl/, because /ʒ/ does not occur in syllable-
final position.

With the exception of /ll/, there is no phonemic gemination
of consonants. (N.B. The geminates [DD], [ss], etc., e.g.
[BiDDĕr] = /bidər/ 'spots, dots', are allophones of the phonemes
/d/ or /s/, respectively.)

Table 12 shows two consonant clusters consisting of a syllable-final and a syllable-initial consonant.

Table 12

Consonant clusters

		Syllable-final consonants									
		10	20	30	40	50	60	70	80	90	100
		b	d	g	m	n	ŋ	s	š	r	l
1	b		•	•	•					•	•
2	m		•							•	•
3	t	•	•	•	•	•	•	•		•	•
4	d	•		•	•	•	•			•	•
5	c	•		•	•	•				•	•
6	ʒ	•		•	•	•				•	•
7	s	•		•	•	•	•			•	•
8	č	•		•	•	•	•	•		•	•
9	ǰ	•		•	•	•				•	•
10	š	•		•	•	•	•			•	•
11	n			•	•			•		•	•
12	l	•	•	•	•			•		•	•
13	r	•		•	•		•	•			
14	g	•			•		•	•	•	•	•
15	x	•	•	•	•		•	•	•	•	•

Syllable-initial consonants

The examples are numbered: the numbers 10 to 100 indicate syllable-final consonants; the numbers 1 to 15 indicate syllable-initial consonants. E.g. in section 10, number 3 refers to the cluster /bt/, etc.

10 /b/ plus another consonant:

3 /dabtəxə/ 'to forge, to do a smith's work', 4 /ebdəxə/ 'to break', 5 /dabcəŋ/ 'platform', 6 /abʒaatae/ 'impermanent, changing', 7 /tabsəg/ 'trunk, large box', 8 /xabčig/ 'narrow', 9 /obǰiŋ/ 'cunning, sly', 10 /ebšeexə/ 'to yawn', 12 /abligə/ 'bribe', 13 /tobruu/ 'anything convex (lens-shaped)', 14 /yabgəŋ/ 'pedestrian', 15 /dabxər/ 'double'

20 /d/ plus another consonant:

1 /udbəl/ 'water lily', 2 /eedməg/ 'sour milk, kind of yogurt', 3 /cadtⱨl/ 'to satiety', 12 /edləxə/ 'to own', 15 /adxə/ 'handful'

30 /g/ plus another consonant:

1 /ӡagbər/ 'pattern', 3 /agtə/ 'gelding', 4/xagdə/ 'last year's dry grass', 5 /bagcə/ 'bundle', 6 /ugӡərxə/ 'to pull, to jerk', 7 /ugsaa/ 'origin, lineage', 8 /agčixə/ 'to dry up and become shorter, to shrink', 9 /negǰixə/ 'to search' (a house, etc.), 10 /ogšixə/ 'to rise', 11 /egnee/ 'ranks', 12 /baglaa/ 'bundle, bunch', 13 /tegrəg/ 'circle, circular', 15 /əgxə/ ~ /əxə/ 'to give'

40 /m/ plus another consonant:

1 /umbəxə/ 'to wade, to walk in water', 3 /xamtə/ 'together', 4 /umdə/ 'drink', 5 /camcə/ 'shirt', 6 /umӡəd/ 'precentor in a Buddhist monastery', 7 /amsəxə/ 'to taste', 8 /əmči/ 'property', 9 /amǰiltə/ 'achievement', 10 /samsuu/ 'digestive organs', 11 /emnəxə/ 'to give medical treatment', 12 /nomləxə/ 'to preach', 13 /amrəg/ 'beloved', 14 /emgəg/ 'ailment', 15 /emxə/ 'order, system'

50 /n/ plus another consonant:

3 /untəxə/ 'to sleep', 4 /endə/ 'here', 5 /xancui/ 'sleeve', 6 /xenӡə/ 'late born', 7 /sansər/ 'material world, world of vanity', 8 /sančig/ 'hair on the temples', 9 /senǰi/ 'eye of a needle', 10 /xonšoor/ 'muzzle, snout'

60 /ŋ/ plus another consonant:

3 /aŋtae/ 'having game animals', 4 /aŋdə/ 'to a game animal', 7 /daŋsə/ 'ledger', 8 /aŋči/ 'trapper, hunter of game', 10 /uŋšixə/ 'to read', 13 /maŋrəxə/ 'to moo', 14 /eŋgər/ 'southern slope', 15 /aŋxə/ 'beginning'

70 /s/ plus another consonant:

3 /tastəxə/ 'to sever, to tear', 8 /ӡesči/ 'coppersmith', 11 /xɯsnəg/ 'form' (document to be filled in), 12 /desləgči/ 'lieutenant', 13 /asrəxə/ 'to take care of somebody', 14 /esgəxə/ 'to cut', 15 /asxəxə/ 'to spill'

80 /š/ plus another consonant:

14 /uušgi/ 'lung', 15 /gišxəxə/ 'to step on'

90 /r/ plus another consonant:

1 /arbəŋ/ 'ten', 2 /erməlʒəxə/ 'to desire', 3 /ertə/ 'early', 4 /erdəm/ 'science, learning', 5 /aarcə/ 'a kind of sour cheese', 6 /garʒə/ 'financial loss', 7 /arsəgər/ 'ramified', 8 /arcixə/ 'to cleanse', 9 /borǰiŋ/ 'granite' (stone), 10 /oršixə/ 'to be in, to dwell', 11 /ərnəxə/ 'to develop', 12 /gerləxə/ 'to marry', 14 /gergii/ 'wife', 15 /barxirəxə/ 'to shout, to yell'

100 /l/ plus another consonant:

1 /albə/ 'service, duty', 2 /balməd/ 'adventurer', 3 /altə/ 'gold', 4 /aldə/ 'fathom', 5 /ulcəŋ/ 'having running eyes', 6 /aalʒə/ 'spider', 7 /elsəg/ 'friendly', 8 /belcixə/ 'to graze', 9 /suɩǰixə/ 'to plait, to knit', 10 /golšig/ 'pleasant, amiable', 11 /xelnə/ 'he says', 12 /emeellə/ 'saddle!', 14 /belgə/ 'sign', 15 / elxəg/ 'sieve'

2.233. Three consonants

Clusters of three consonants may appear in fast speech as a result of elision of /ə/. The first component of such clusters is /n l r/.

/uɩnsənees/ > /uɩnsnees/ 'from cinders'
/altənaas/ > /altnaas/ 'from gold'
/xulsənaas/ > /xulsnaas/ 'from reeds'
/orsənoos/ > /orsnoos/ 'from having entered'

2.3. Morphophonemics

This section deals with the alternation of nasals, the alternation of vowels, and internal and external sandhi.

2.31. Alternation of nasals

The phoneme /n/ does not occur in final position. In fast
speech, a final shwa may be dropped, leaving a preceding /n/
in final position. However, such a final /n/ is phonemically
/nə/. Only /ŋ/ occurs in absolute final position.

Final /ŋ/ is, historically, of dual origin. In some words
it goes back to *ŋ; in others, it has developed from *n, e.g.
/aŋ/ < *aŋ 'game animal', but /oŋ/ < *on 'year'.

When final /ŋ/ goes back to *ŋ, it always retains its velar
articulation. Moreover, it even becomes /ŋg/ before a vowel,
e.g. /aŋ/ 'game animal', /aŋ+də/ 'to the game animal', /aŋg+aas/
'from the game animal'.

When final /ŋ/ goes back to *n, it again becomes /n/ when
a suffix beginning with a vowel or a consonant other than a
velar consonant is added, e.g. /oŋ/ 'year', but /on+də/ 'in the
year', /on+oos/ 'from the year', etc. In such stems, there is
an alternation /ŋ/~/n/. Such stems are called "stems with a
stable /n/".

There is a large group of nouns with stems ending in /n/
which retain this /n/ in some positions, but drop it in other
positions, e.g. /temeen+/ 'camel': /temee/ 'camel' (subject
form), /temee+g/ 'camel' (dir. obj.), /temeen+də/ 'to the camel',
/temeen+ees/ 'from the camel'. Such stems are called "stems with
an unstable /n/".

Consequently, there are three distinct classes of stems:
1. Stems with alternating /ŋ/~/ŋg/
2. Stems with alternating /ŋ/~/n/
3. Stems with alternating /n/~zero
Examples: 1. /aŋ/~/aŋg+/ 'game animal', 2. /noyəŋ/~/noyən+/
'prince', 3. /modən+/~/modə/ 'tree'. The presence of /+/ indicates that the form in question is the stem, and the absence of /+/
indicates that the form is the subject form.

2.32. Alternation of vowels

2.321. Regular alternation of /ə/ with zero is found in cases in
which a geminate vowel other than /ii/ is added to a stem-final
/ə/, the result being that /ə/ is absorbed by the geminate
vowel or, so to speak, "disappears", e.g. /axə+/ 'elder brother'
+ /aar/ instrumental → /axaar/ 'by means of the elder brother'.

2.322. In cases in which /ii/ is added to a stem-final /ə/, the
/ə/ remains, and, together with /ii/, becomes /əii/, i.e. [ī]
with a preceding shwa glide, the allophone of the shwa depending
on the quality of the vowel of the preceding syllable, e.g.
/axə+/ 'elder brother' + /iiŋ/ genitive → /axəiiŋ/ 'of the elder
brother'; /xotə+/ 'city' + /iiŋ/ → /xotəiiŋ/ 'of the city';
/bexə+/ 'wrestler' + /iiŋ/ → /bexəiiŋ/ 'of the wrestler'.

2.323. Regular alternation of stem-final /i/ with zero is found
in cases in which geminate /ii/ is added. When /i/, so to
speak, "disappears", its remaining trace is the palatalization
of an immediately preceding /l m n r/, e.g. /surguuli/ 'school'
+ /iiŋ/ → /surguuliiŋ/ [surg͜ūlʲĪ˷] 'of the school'; /ami/
'life' + /iiŋ/ → /amiiŋ/ [ámʲĪ˷] 'of the life'.

2.324. Regular alternation of stem-final /i/ with zero occurs also
when any geminate vowel phoneme (not necessarily /ii/) is added
to a stem in which stem-final /i/ is preceded by /š č ǰ/, e.g.
/bagši+/ 'teacher' + /aar/ instrumental → /bagšaar/ 'by means
of the teacher'; /surəgči+/ 'student' + /aar/ → /surəgčaar/ 'by
means of the student'; /argəmǰi/ 'rope' + /aar/ → /argəmǰaar/
'by means of a rope'.

2.325. A regular alternation of /ə/ and /i/ with zero occurs in
the final closed syllable of a disyllabic stem when a geminate
vowel or a diphthong is added. This occurs in words in which
/ə/ or /i/ is preceded by /l m̥ n r/ or /s/, e.g. /usən+/ 'water'
+ /aas/ ablative → /usnaas/ 'from water'; /bilig+/ 'intellect' +

/eer/ instrumental → /bilgeer/ 'by means of the intellect';
/xulsən+/ 'reed' + /aas/ → /xulsnaas/ 'from reed'; /olsən+/
'hemp rope' + /oos/ → /olsnoos/ 'from hemp rope'.

2.326. An irregular and rather unpredictable alternation of /ə/
or /i/ with zero occurs in fast speech. These two vowel phonemes may be dropped in final position, or disappear in medial
position, e.g. /enə xɯŋ ulaambaatəraas irsəŋ/ 'this man has
come from Ulan Bator' may be pronounced in slow speech, in which
all words are pronounced carefully and with clear intervals between them, as [énĕ xɯŋ u̯lā̆~ bāt^hărās irsĕ~], but it may also be
pronounced as [én xɯŋ u̯lâmbāt^hrās irsĕ~]. In fast speech, therefore, it is by no means easy to divide a Mongolian word into
syllables and to establish their boundaries. Thus, [arwă~] 'ten',
in fast speech, could be interpreted as /arəbəŋ/ or as /arbəŋ/.
A word like [xəDDĕlmĕrč^hĭ~] could be interpreted as /xədəlmərčiŋ/
or as /xədləmərčiŋ/ or /xədəlmərəčiŋ/ or /xədləmərəčiŋ/.

There occurs also irregular metathesis of the shwa between
a liquid and another consonant, e.g. /xaalgə/~/xaaləg/ 'gate',
/argə/~/arəg/ 'means', /belgə/~/beləg/ 'sign, omen', etc.

Matters are made easier when one keeps in mind that /p č ǰ
t c ʒ y k x/ do not occur in syllable-final position. Consequently, [ut^hsār] 'by means of thread' in fast speech cannot be
/utsaar/ but can only be /utəsaar/. In other words, any of these
nine consonants always presumes a following vowel, and syllable-
final /p č ǰ t c ʒ y k x/ can only be /pV čV ǰV tV cV ʒV yV kV
xV/, where V is either /ə/ or /i/.

In syllable-final position only /b d g s š m n ŋ l r/ occur.
Therefore, the really difficult cases are those in which a vowel
may have been dropped after one of these consonants, excluding,
however, /ŋ/, which never occurs before vowels. This is so because both /bCV dCV gCV/, etc., and /bVCV dVCV gVCV/, etc., are
possible, C being any other consonant, and V being any vowel,
e.g. /xabətae/ 'having skill, skillful' and /xabtae/ 'having a
Pekinese'; or /bagətae/ 'having something in a small quantity'

and /bagtae/ 'possessing a bag' (i.e. an administrative unit of
a few households). Street has demonstrated that there is a
clear contrast between the presence or absence of /ə/ after
/b g s m n l r/, to which /d/, not mentioned by him, should also
be added.

2.33. Internal sandhi

Internal sandhi manifests itself in the assimilation or alternation of consonants within a word.

2.331. Assimilation manifests itself in the occurrence of different allophones in various positions, e.g. syllable-final /b g
l r/ are unvoiced before /t c č s š x/ and represented by the
allophones [B Ģ G L R] respectively, i.e. the alternations
[b]~[B], etc., are nonphonemic.

2.332. Alternation manifests itself in the choice of allomorphs
of certain morphemes, namely, those having /d ǰ g/ at their onset.

Table 12 shows all the two-consonant clusters that occur
in Mongolian. Not all of them, however, occur at morpheme
boundaries. For example, /bd/ is possible within a morpheme,
e.g. /ebdə-/ 'to break', but /bd/ does not occur at morpheme
boundaries, i.e. a morpheme beginning with /d/ cannot be added
to a morpheme ending in /b/. Also, when /g r/ are in morpheme-
final position, no /d/ can be added. Further, as was seen
above, the clusters /dd sd/ do not occur at all; therefore, no
/d/ can be added to a morpheme which has final /d s/.

2.3321. Suffixes with initial /d/ are the dative-locative suffix
and the passive-verb suffix.

The dative-locative suffix is /də/, e.g. /xaan+/ 'king',
/xaandə/ 'to the king'. With stems ending in /b d g s r/, the
allomorph /tə/ is used.

/teləb+/ 'form', /teləbtə/ 'to the form'
/boləd+/ 'steel', /bolədtə/ 'to the steel'
/bičig+/ 'letter', /bičigtə/ 'to the letter'
/uləs+/ 'nation', /uləstə/ 'to the nation'
/gar+/ 'hand', /gartə/ 'to the hand'

The passive-verb suffix is /də-/, e.g. /ol-/ 'to find', /oldə-/ 'to be found'. With stems ending in /b g s r/, the allomorph /tə-/ is used.

/ab-/ 'to take', /abtə-/ 'to be taken'
/eg-/ 'to give', /egtə-/ 'to be given'
/gar-/ 'to overtake', /gartə-/ 'to be overtaken'

2.3322. The suffix of the imperfect gerund is /ǰi/, e.g. /ol-/ 'to find', /olǰi/ 'finding'. With verbal stems ending in /b g s r/, the allomorph /či/ is used.

/ab-/ 'to take', /abči/ 'taking'
/eg-/ 'to give', /egči/ 'giving'
/bos-/ 'to rise', /bosči/ 'rising'
/gar-/ 'to overtake', /garči/ 'overtaking'

2.3323. The suffix of the causative verb is /gə-/. In Ordos and some other dialects there are two allomorphs, /gE-/ and /xE-/; when the stem of the verb ends in /b s/, the allomorph /xE-/ is used. Some subdialects of Khalkha also have two allomorphs, /gə-/ and /xə-/, but the new literary language is based on a dialect which has only /gə-/, e.g. Ordos /bos-/ 'to rise', /bosxo-/ 'to raise'; North Khalkha /bos-/ 'to rise', /bosxə-/ 'to raise'; Standard Khalkha /bosgə-/ 'to raise'.

2.34. <u>External sandhi</u>

External sandhi manifests itself in assimilation of consonants belonging to different words, e.g. one consonant being word-final and the next one word-initial. This occurs in fast speech. Either the preceding consonant is assimilated to the succeeding consonant or <u>vice versa</u>.

2.341. The preceding consonant is assimilated to the succeeding
one.

(a) Final /ŋ/. When the next consonant is /b/ or /m/,
word-final /ŋ/ becomes /m/, e.g. /saeŋ baenə/ [säɛ̈m bäɛ̈nä]
'is good'.

When the next consonant is a dental, word-final /ŋ/ becomes
/n/, e.g. /ulaaŋ tug/ [u̯lān tʰuG] 'red banner'; /meŋgeŋ ʒoos/
[meŋgĕn ʒōs] 'silver coin'.

(b) Final /ǰ/ of the gerund is replaced by /d/ before a
following /s/.

/xelǰ baenə/ 'is speaking'

/xelǰ suub/ [xelD sūw] 'sat speaking, sat and spoke'.

2.342. The succeeding consonant is assimilated in voicing to the
preceding word-final consonant. This affects only /b/ following
/m n ŋ l/ and /g/ following /m n ŋ l r/. In isolation, /b/ in
/baenə/ 'is' is [B], but in /saeŋ baenə/ [säɛ̈m bäɛ̈nä] 'is good',
it is [b].

The same can be said, <u>mutatis mutandis</u>, about /g/.

2.4. Orthographical representation of the phonemes

2.41. General remarks on the alphabet

The new Mongolian (Cyrillic) alphabet is not phonemic. It lacks
specific graphemes for some phonemes, e.g. /y/ and /ə/, and in
some cases uses one letter for two phonemes, e.g. я = /ya/.
On the other hand, one letter sometimes renders different phonemes, e.g. e , which is /ye/ in some cases but /yə/ in other
cases, and /y/ in a third group of cases. Consequently, the
phonemic value of some graphemes is not immediately predictable.

2.42. Representation of the consonant phonemes

The consonants б and в represent /b/. The allophones [b] and
[B] are rendered with б , the allophones [w] and [W] are rendered
with в .

The following letters render their respective phonemes quite adequately, i.e. each letter denotes only one consonant phoneme:

г	/g/	к	/k/	р	/r/	х	/x/
д	/d/	л	/l/	с	/s/	ц	/c/
ж	/ǰ/	м	/m/	т	/t/	ч	/č/
з	/ʒ/	п	/p/	ф	/f/	ш	/š/

N.B. In final position, the letters **ж ч ш** render /ǰi či ši/ respectively.

The letter **н** is ambiguous because it represents both /n/ and /ŋ/. Initially and intervocalically, it is /n/, but in word-final position and before /g x/ (and /k/ in loan words), it represents /ŋ/. The orthography is completely ambiguous in the cases of the clusters /nd ŋd nt ŋt nč ŋč/ because, in all of them, /n/ and /ŋ/ are rendered with **н**.

анд	/andə/ 'friend' and /aŋdə/ 'to a game animal'
анч	/aŋč/ 'hunter'
онч	/onči/ 'inertia'
санд	/sandə/ in /sandə mendə/ 'in a hurry' and /saŋdə/ 'in the treasury'
банк	/baŋk/ 'bank'

The letters **т** and **г** render /t/ and /g/ in all cases but one: the cluster /dx/ is written as **тг**, e.g. **хатгах** /xadxəxə/ 'to sting'.

2.43. Representation of the vowel phonemes

The single vowel phonemes (with the exception of /i/) and the geminate vowel phonemes are rendered in a uniform manner: one letter stands for a single vowel phoneme, and the repetition of the same letter is used to render the geminate vowel phoneme.

хана	/xanə/ 'wall'
хаана	/xaanə/ 'where?'

The orthographical representation of the diphthongs is simple: the non-syllabic element in /ae oe ui ɯi/ is always rendered with **й**.

сайн /saeŋ/ 'good'

ой /oe/ 'forest'

уйлах /uiləxə/ 'to weep'

The general principle is to avoid groups of more than two vowel letters. Therefore /iaa/ is **иа** . To avoid confusion of /iaa/ with /ia/, the latter is rendered with **я**

мянган /miaŋgəŋ/ 'thousand'

амиараа /amiaaraa/ 'apart, separately'

2.431. Representation of /i/

The phoneme /i/ is regularly rendered by **и** , and in certain non-initial syllables by **ь** . The letter **ь** represents /i/ in final position after /m n l r g b t d x/, provided that the consonant is preceded by a vowel but not by another consonant, i.e. **ь** is not written after consonant clusters. In medial position **ь** represents /i/ when it occurs between a consonant of Group I and a consonant of Group II or a convocalic.

Consonants of Group I: **б в г л м н р**

Consonants of Group II: **д ж з с т х ц ч ш**

Convocalics: **е ё ю я**

тань /tani/ 'recognize!'

харь /xari/ 'stranger'

тоть /toti/ 'parrot'

захь /ẑaxi/ 'place an order!'

амьд /amidə/ 'live, living'

тольд /tolidə/ 'in the mirror'

харьяат /xariyaatə/ 'subject of a country'

In all the other cases **и** is used.

тамхи /tamxi/ 'tobacco'

тотид /totidə/ 'to the parrot'

ажил /ajil/ 'work'

The geminate vowel phoneme /ii/ is rendered with **ий**.

ийм /iimə/ 'such'

хийснэ /xiisənə/ 'flies in the wind'

дэлхий /delxii/ 'world'

амийг /amiig/ 'the life' (dir. obj.)

багшийг /bagšiig/ 'the teacher' (dir. obj.)

2.432. The phoneme /əii/

The phoneme /əii/, which occurs only in noninitial syllables, is always rendered with **ы** .

амын /aməiiŋ/ 'of the mouth'

гарыг /garəiig/ 'the hand' (dir. obj.)

2.433. Representation of shwa

The overshort, reduced vowel phoneme /ə/ is indicated in some positions but is not marked in others. Where it is indicated, it is rendered with the letters **а о э ө** , which render rather accurately the allophones of /ə/ = [ă ŏ ĕ ŏ̈]; or with **ъ** , which is used only before syllables with **ё я** /yoo yaa/.

оръё /orəyoo/ 'let us enter!'

гаръя /garəyaa/ 'let us go out!'

очъё /očəyoo/ 'let us go!'

The principal rules regarding the letters **а о э ө** are shown in Table 13.

Table 13

Representation of /ə/

After syllables with:	/ə/ is written with:
а аа ай у уу уй	**а**
о оо ой	**о**
э ээ ү үү үй	**э**
ө өө	**ө**

бага	/bagə/	'small'
байна	/baenə/	'is'
хаана	/xaanə/	'where?'
унах	/unəxə/	'to fall down'
ууна	/uunə/	'he drinks'
уйлах	/uiləxə/	'to weep'
модонд	/modəndə/	'in the forest'
оосор	/oosər/	'tape'
хойно	/xoenə/	'afterwards'
эвлэл	/ebləl/	'union'
үнэн	/ɯnəŋ/	'truth'
өргөн	/ərgəŋ/	'wide, broad'

The rules of Mongolian orthography require that a consonant of
Group I must either have a vowel letter preceding it or following, whereas a consonant of Group II needs no vowel preceding it
or following it when this consonant comes immediately after a
consonant of Group I or when it is between two consonants of
Group I, one of which is preceded and the other is followed by
a vowel. In other words, the vowel (V) must be indicated only
either before or after a consonant of Group I (CI). Consequently, /yabəgəŋ/ 'pedestrian' can only be written as **явган**
because /b/, which is a consonant of Group I, is preceded by a
vowel and therefore no vowel is written after it. Likewise,
/maltəməl/ 'soil deposits' can only be written as **малтмал**
because /t/ is between two consonants of Group I, one of which
is preceded and the other is followed by a vowel, i.e. after
/t/ no vowel is written, because /t/ follows CVCI and is followed by CIVC. The formula for this word is CIVCICIICIVCI.

2.44. The convocalics

The Mongolian Cyrillic alphabet has four letters which represent
syllables consisting of /y/ followed by a vowel. These are
е ё ю я.

  е renders both /ye/ and /yə/ initially, and /yə/ in noninitial syllables. In monosyllables, /ye/ and /yə/ are not

distinguished from each other. The combination **eэ** renders
/yee/. When **e** is followed by a vowel letter other than **э** or **ө**,
it renders /y/. Note that **e** renders /-yee/ or /-yөe/ in the
voluntative suffix.

ep	/yer/	'ninety' (as noun)
ep	/yər/	'in general'
epэн	/yerəŋ/	'ninety' (as adjective)
epөн	/yərəŋ/	'in general'
бие	/biyə/	'body'
биейн	/biyiiŋ/	'of the body'
биеэ	/biyee/	'oneself' (dir. obj.)
хэлье	/xeləyee/	'I shall say'

ё renders /yo/ initially, and /yə/ in noninitial syllables.
The combination **ёo** renders /yoo/. Note that **ё** renders /-yoo/
in the voluntative suffix.

ёc	/yos/	'custom'
гоё	/goyə/	'pretty, elegant'
оёoc	/oyoos/	'seam'
оръё	/orəyoo/	'let us enter!'

ю renders both /yu/ and /yɯ/ initially. In monosyllables,
/yu/ and /yɯ/ are not distinguished from each other. The combination **юy** renders /yuu/, and the combination **юY** renders
/yɯɯ/.

юм	/yum/	'something'
юлд	/yɯldə/	'herpes'
юунд	/yuundə/	'why?'
буюу	/buyuu/	'or'
юмбYY	/yɯmbɯɯ/	'bullion'

я renders /ya/ at the beginning of a word, /ia/ in an
initial syllable beginning with a consonant, and /yə/ in noninitial syllables. The combination **яa** renders /yaa/. Note
that **я** renders /-yaa/ in the voluntative suffix.

явах	/yabəxə/	'to go'
мянган	/miaŋgəŋ/	'thousand'

ая	/ayə/ 'circumstance'
баян	/bayəŋ/ 'rich'
яасан	/yaasəŋ/ 'what kind of?'
явъя	/yabəyaa/ 'let us go!'

2.45. The postconsonantals

The postconsonantals are **ъ** and **ь** . The letter **ъ** is called the "hard sign". Its function in Mongolian orthography is to render /ə/ or zero.

    авъя   /abəyaa/ or /abyaa/ 'let us take!'

The letter **ь** is the so-called "soft sign". It indicates the phoneme /i/, or zero.

2.46. Summary of the graphemes

The following list shows all the graphemes of Mongolian, with indication of phonemic values and with examples.

SUMMARY OF THE GRAPHEMES OF MONGOLIAN

Grapheme	Phonemic Value	Position	Examples		
a	/a/	Initial syllable	тах	/taxe/	'horseshoe'
	/e/	Noninitial syllables	арван	/arbeŋ/	'ten'
aa	/aa/	All syllables	нааш	/naaši/	'hither'
ай	/ae/	All syllables	сайн	/saeŋ/	'good'
б	/b/	Initial; medial after л м н	бар	/bar/	'tiger'
			алба	/albe/	'service'
в	/b/	Final and medial after consonants other than л м н; intervocalic	ав	/ab/	'take!'
			татвар	/tateber/	'tax'
г	/g/	All positions	гал	/gal/	'fire'
д	/d/	All positions	дотор	/doter/	'inside'
е	/ye/	Initial	ер	/yer/	'ninety'
	/ye/	Initial	есөн	/yesen/	'nine'
	/ye/	After a vowel	бие	/biye/	'body'
	/yee/	Voluntative suffix	нээе	/neeyee/	'let us open!'
	/yee/	Same after ө	өгье	/egeyee/	'let us give!'
	/y/	Before vowels other than э or ө	биейн	/biyiŋ/	'of the body'

Grapheme	Phonemic Value	Position	Examples		
ез	/yee/	Initial; after vowels и з ү	ез	/yee/	excl. of disappointment
			биез	/biyee/	'himself' (dir. obj.)
ё	/yo/	Initial	ёс	/yos/	'custom'
	/yə/	In noninitial syllables	оёх	/oyəx/	'to sew'
	/yoo/	Voluntative suffix	оръё	/orəyoo/	'let us go in!'
ёо	/yoo/	Initial and medial	ёоз	/yooz/	'deuce'
			оёор	/oyoor/	'bottom'
ёу	/yuu/	Noninitial syllables	хоёул	/xoyuul/	'both'
ж	/ǰ/	All positions	жил	/ǰil/	'year'
з	/ʒ/	All positions	зах	/ʒaxə/	'edge'
и	/i/	Initial and noninitial syllables	ир	/ir/	'come!'
			амжилт	/amǰiltə/	'achievement'
ий	/yi/	Initial in some words	их	/yixə/	'large'
ийм	/ii/	All positions	ийм	/iimə/	'such'
иа	/iaa/	Noninitial syllables	ханиад	/xaniaadə/	'cough'
ио	/ioo/	Noninitial syllables	хориод	/xoriood/	'about twenty'

Cyrillic	IPA	Position / Environment	Example	Transcription	Gloss
иу	/iuu/	Noninitial syllables	хариу	/xariuu/	'answer'
й	/e/	In /ae oe/	сайн	/saeŋ/	'good'
			нохой	/noxoe/	'dog'
	/i/	In /ui ɯi/	уйлах	/uilɛx/	'to weep'
			үйл	/ɯilə/	'work'
к	/k/	All positions (in loan words)	консул	/koonsəl/	'consul'
л	/l/	All positions	лам	/lam/	'priest'
м	/m/	All positions	мал	/mal/	'cattle'
н	/n/	Initial; between vowels; in most cases before consonants other than г х	нар	/nar/	'sun'
			энэ	/ene/	'this'
			энд	/ende/	'here'
	/ŋ/	Word-final; before г х; sometimes before other consonants	хүүхэн	/xɯɯxəŋ/	'girl'
			онгоц	/oŋgəc/	'boat'
			анх	/aŋxə/	'beginning'
			анд	/aŋdə/	'to the game animal'
о	/o/	Initial syllable	он	/oŋ/	'year'
	/ə/	Noninitial syllables	оронд	/orəndə/	'in the place'
оо	/oo/	All syllables	оосор	/oosər/	'tape'

Grapheme	Phonemic Value	Position	Examples	
ой	/oe/	All syllables	ой	/oe/ 'forest'
ө	/ə/	Initial syllable	өндөр	/əndər/ 'high'
	/ө/	Noninitial syllables	хөтөл	/xətəl/ 'hill'
өө	/əə/	All syllables	өөрөө	/əərəə/ 'himself'
п	/p/	All positions (in loan words)	пүрэв	/pʊrbə/ 'Thursday'
			опер	/oopir/ 'opera'
р	/r/	All positions	рам	/ram/ 'indigo'
с	/s/	All positions	сар	/sar/ 'moon'
т	/t/	All syllables	татах	/tatəx/ 'to pull'
			хотгор	/xotəgər/ 'soil depression'
тг	/dx/	At syllable boundary	атга	/adxə/ 'handful'
у	/u/	Initial syllable	ус	/us/ 'water'
уу	/uu/	All syllables	уул	/uul/ 'mountain'
уа	/uaa/	All syllables	гуа	/guaa/ 'beautiful woman'
уай	/uae/	Initial syllable	гуай	/guae/ 'Mr.'
уй	/ui/	All syllables	уйлах	/uiləx/ 'to weep'

Letter	Value	Position	Example
у	/u/	Initial syllable	ус /us/ 'hair'
уу	/uu/	All syllables	ууд /uudə/ 'door'
үй	/ui/	All syllables	үйл /uilə/ 'work'
ф	/f/	All positions (in loan words)	фабрик /faabrikə/ 'factory'
х	/x/	All positions	хатуу /xatuu/ 'hard'
ц	/c/	All positions	цаг /cag/ 'time'
ч	/č/	All positions	чи /či/ 'thou'
ш	/š/	All positions	шинэ /šinə/ 'new'
ъ	/ə/~zero	Medial before the letters ё я	орьё /orəyoo/ 'let us go in!' ; явья /yabəyaa/ 'let us go!'
ы	/əii/	Noninitial syllables in words with back vowels	галын /galəiiŋ/ 'of the fire'
ь	/i/	Final after г д л м н р т х; medial between CI and CII	толь /toli/ 'mirror' ; амьд /amidə/ 'living'
	zero	Between CI and convocalic	ирье /iryee/ 'let us come!'
э	/e/	Initial syllable	энэ /enə/ 'this'
э	/ə/	Noninitial syllables	үнэ /unə/ 'price'
ээ	/ee/	All syllables	дээрээс /deerees/ 'from above'

Grapheme	Phonemic Value	Position	Examples
ЭЙ	/ee/	In the suffix /tee/ **ТЭЙ**	**ГЭРТЭЙ** /gertee/ 'having a house; married'
Ю	/yu/	Initial syllable in words with back vowels	юмаар /yumaar/ 'by means of something'
ЮБҮҮ	/yʉ/	Initial syllable in words with front vowels	**ЮМБҮҮ** /yʉmbʉʉ/ 'bullion'
ЮУ	/yuu/	All syllables of words with back vowels	**ЮУГААР** /yuugaar/ 'by means of what?'
ЮҮ	/yʉʉ/	All syllables of words with front vowels	**ЮҮЛЭХ** /yʉʉlxə/ 'to transfuse'
Я	/ya/	Initial	**ЯВАХ** /yabəxə/ 'to go'
я	/yə/	Noninitial syllables	баян /bayəŋ/ 'rich'
я	/ia/	Initial syllable after a consonant	МЯНГАН /miaŋgəŋ/ 'thousand'
ЯЬ	/yaa/	Voluntative suffix	**ЯВЬЯА** /yabəyaa/ 'let us go!'
ЯВ	/yaa/	Initial; medial after a vowel	**ЯСАН** /yaasəŋ/ 'what kind of?' аяархан /ayaarxəŋ/ 'still, careful'
ЯЙ	/yae/	Initial	**ЯЙРАХ** /yaerəxə/ 'to crumble'

2.5. Select Bibliography

Bosson, J., and Unensečen, B., "Some Notes on the Dialect of the Khorchin Mongols", American Studies in Altaic Linguistics (= Uralic and Altaic Series, Vol. 13), Bloomington, Indiana, 1962, pp. 23-44.

Hattori, S., "Phonemic Structure of Mongol (Chakhar Dialect)", Journal of the Linguistic Society of Japan 19-20 (1951), pp. 68-102.

Mostaert, A., "Le dialecte des mongols Urdus (sud)", Anthropos 21-22 (1926-1927).

Nomura, M., "On Some Phonological Developments in the Kharachin Dialect", Studia Altaica, Wiesbaden, 1957, pp. 132-136.

Ramstedt, G.J., "Das Schriftmongolische und die Urgamundart phonetisch verglichen", Journal de la Société Finno-Ougrienne 21:2 (1903), pp. 1-55. (An excellent phonetic description of Khalkha and comparison with Script Mongolian.)

Róna-Tas, A., "A Study of Dariganga Phonology", Acta Orientalia Hungarica 10:1 (1960), pp. 1-29.

Street, J.C., Khalkha Structure (= Uralic and Altaic Series, Vol. 24), Bloomington, Indiana, 1963. (An excellent and highly recommended work on Khalkha, particularly pp. 1-79, which deal with phonology and problems of morphophonemics and the Cyrillic alphabet.)

-----, "Urdus Phonology: A Restatement", Ural-Altaische Jahrbücher 38 (1966), pp. 92-111.

-----, "Kalmyk Shwa", American Studies in Altaic Linguistics (= Uralic and Altaic Series, Vol. 13), Bloomington, Indiana, 1962, pp. 263-291.

Vladimircov, B. Ya., Sravnitel'naya grammatika mongol'skogo pis'mennogo yazïka i xalxaskogo narečiya, Leningrad, 1929. (Pp. 51-91 contain a phonetic description of Khalkha. Although obsolete as a whole, the book is still of value because of the vast amount of material presented.)

3. MORPHOLOGY

3.1. Typological structure

3.11. Agglutination

Mongolian is an agglutinative language, i.e. word formation and
inflection are carried out by attaching one morpheme to another,
e.g. a suffix to a stem. (The process is called "agglutination",
from the Latin verb agglutinare 'to glue to'.) Except for the
morphophonemic alternations and internal sandhi discussed in
section 2.3, the elements "glued" to one another do not undergo
any change.

3.12. Stems and suffixes

All Mongolian morphemes can be divided into two groups: stems
and suffixes. A stem is a lexical morpheme; it is, so to speak,
the carrier of the basic meaning, e.g. /ger+/ 'house', /gar+/
'hand', /gal+/ 'fire', etc. A suffix is an element which does
not convey any lexical meaning and does not occur alone. It
changes the meaning of the stem or gives its meaning another
nuance. A suffix does not occur freely. Whereas /ger/ 'house'
or /gal/ 'fire' may occur freely and without any suffix, a suffix, such as /+gči/ of the actor, does not occur freely but only
after another morpheme, i.e. the stem.

Stems are primary and derived. A primary stem consists of
only one morpheme, e.g. /ger+/ 'house'. It cannot be reduced
to any smaller morphological unit. But another stem may be
derived from a primary stem. Thus, by adding /+lə-/, which
derives verbs from nouns, the derived secondary stem /gerlə-/
'to marry' may be formed. (At first glance, 'marry' has nothing
in common with the word for house. However, it originated from
the idea of 'to make a home of one's own'.) By adding other

74

suffixes of derivation, e.g. /-ɯɯl-/, other words may be formed from /gerlə-/ 'to marry'; cf. /gerlɯɯl-/ 'to make marry' which is a tertiary stem.

Suffixes can be divided into two groups: derivational and inflectional. The derivational suffixes form new stems, e.g. /+lə-/ (cf. /ger+lə-/ 'to marry', from /ger/ 'house, home'). The inflectional suffixes yield different forms of the same word. The suffixes of noun declension and of verb conjugation are inflectional suffixes.

It follows from the above that words may consist of a number of morphemes, namely, a stem and several suffixes, e.g.:

/bari-/ 'to seize'
/bari-ldə-/ 'to seize each other' (= 'to wrestle')
/bari-ld-aa/ 'the wrestling'
/bari-ld-aa+či/ 'wrestler'
/bari-ld-aa+či+d/ 'wrestlers'
/bari-ld-aa+či+d+tə/ 'to the wrestlers'

As stated above, the stem occurs freely. This applies to both primary and derived stems. The stem of a noun is the subject-direct object case, e.g. /ger+/ 'house'. The stem of a verb is the imperative, second person singular, e.g. /suu-/ 'sit down!'

A derived stem, i.e. secondary, tertiary, etc., can always be traced to a primary stem. However, in a few cases, no part of a word can be identified as its primary stem. For example, the words /enə/ 'this', /edə/ 'these' (cf. /terə/ 'that' and /tedə/ 'those') have in common the initial element /e+/, which does not occur freely. Such an element may be called a root. Other examples are: /deerə/ 'on', /deeši/ 'upwards', /deedə/ 'upper', /deegɯɯr/ 'along the top', which have the morpheme /dee+/ in common, which does not occur freely. There are also verbs, e.g. /xəldə-/ 'to freeze, to congeal', /xər-/ 'to become cold', /xəši-/ 'to become stiff with cold', all three derived from /xə-/, which does not occur freely. In practical grammars,

roots are not discussed, because the stems derived from them
are treated as independent entities, just as a grammar of
Modern English would not discuss the historical relationship
between words like think and thank.

The suffixes, with a very few exceptions, comply with the
rules of vowel harmony, i.e. a suffix may appear with different
vowels, depending on the vowels of the preceding syllables.
Consequently, all suffixes can be divided into the following
groups, depending on the number of different forms in which the
suffix in question occurs.

(1) One form:

Suffixes with /ii/, e.g. /+ii/ of the genitive, e.g.
/xelnii/ 'of the tongue', /morinii/ 'of the horse'.

Suffixes with /ə/, e.g. /+də/ of the dative-locative, e.g.
/xendə/ 'to whom?', /axədə/ 'to the elder brother'.

(2) Two forms:

Suffixes with /uɯ/, e.g. /-uɯl-/ of causative verbs, e.g.
/meduɯl-/ 'to let know', /yabuul-/ 'to let go, to send away'.

(3) Four forms:

Suffixes with /ee/, e.g. /+eer/ of the instrumental, e.g.
/tergeer/ 'by car', /xeleer/ 'by means of the foot', /garaar/
'by hand', /modoor/ 'by means of a stick'.

3.2. Form and functional classes

Mongolian word classes are distinguished by a combination of
formal and functional criteria. There are ten classes of stems,
namely, nouns, adjectives, numerals, pronouns, adverbs, postpositions, verbs, conjunctions, particles, and interjections.

3.21. Nouns

Nouns may occur with all the suffixes given under noun inflection
(see 3.41) and may act as subjects in clauses and as direct objects in verbal phrases. They may also act as heads of nominal
phrases. There are several sub-classes of nouns, as follows.

3.211. The negative noun /ɯgɯi/ 'absence, nonexistence', which
can be declined and occurs with postpositions, e.g. /ɯgɯiŋ/
'of the nonexistence', /ɯgɯidə/ 'in the absence', /ɯgɯigee/
'his own absence' (dir. obj.), /ɯgɯiŋ tul/ 'because of the
absence'.

3.212. The reflexive nouns /eer/ 'self' and /eersəd/ 'selves',
which occur only with the reflexive suffix when functioning as
subject of a clause, e.g. /eeree/ 'oneself', /eersədee/ 'selves',
/eertee/ 'to himself', /eersədtee/ 'to themselves', /eeriiŋ/
'of himself', /eersədiiŋ/ 'ot themselves, their own', /oersədiiŋ
tul/ 'for their own sake'.

3.213. The interrogative nouns /xen+/ 'who?' and /yuu/ (stem
/yuun+/) 'what?', which are declined as any other noun but have
no plural, e.g. /xenii/ 'of whom?' = 'whose?', /xendə/ 'to
whom?', /yuugaar/ 'by means of what?'.

3.214. The indefinite nouns are based on the interrogative nouns
given above and are formed with the particle /č/, which follows
any inflectional suffix, e.g. /xenč/ 'whoever, anyone', /xeniič/
'anyone's', /xendəč/ 'to anyone'; /yuuč/ 'whatever, anything'
(stem /yuun+/), /yuuniič/ 'of anything', /yuugaarč/ 'by means
of anything'.

3.22. Adjectives

Adjectives are used as attributes in attribute-plus-head nominal
phrases, e.g. /saeŋ xɯndə/ 'to a good person'. They also occur
in phrases which correspond, in meaning, to the comparative and
superlative constructions of English, e.g. /narnaas xaluuŋ/
'hotter than the sun', /xamgiiŋ saeŋ/ 'the best', lit. 'the good
of all'. Adjectives occur with adverbs and intensifying particles, e.g. /toŋ buruu/ 'absolutely wrong', /šab šar/ 'completely yellow'. Many adjectives function as adverbs and occur
preverbally, e.g. /saeŋ medənə/ 'he knows well'.

Adjectives are declined when substantivized, e.g. /saenəiig/ 'the good one' (dir. obj.), /saendaa/ 'in his goodness', /saenin/ 'his good one'.

3.221. The demonstrative adjectives are /iimə/ 'one like this', /tiimə/ 'one like that', /edɯi/ 'this much, as many as these', /tedɯi/ 'that much, as many as those'.

When functioning as nouns, the demonstrative adjectives are declined and occur with postpositions, e.g. /iimiiŋ/ 'of one like this, of such one', /tiimiiŋ tul/ 'because of one like that, because of such one', /tedɯigees/ 'from that much'.

3.222. The interrogative adjectives are /yamər/ 'what, what kind of?', /ali/ 'which?', /xedəŋ/ 'how many?'.

When functioning as a noun, the adjective /xedəŋ/ drops its final /ŋ/, e.g. /xedəŋ xɯŋ/ 'how many people?'; but /xedə baenə/ 'how many are there?'.

The interrogative noun /yuun+/ (see 3.213) functions as an adjective, appearing in the adjective form /yuuŋ/, e.g. /yuuŋ xɯŋ/ 'what kind of a person?'.

3.223. The indefinite adjectives are based on the interrogative adjectives. Some of them are formed with the particle /č/ (cf. 3.214), e.g. /yamərč/ 'whatever', /alinč/ 'whichever', /alibaa/ 'any' < Script Mongolian.

3.23. Numerals

The cardinal numerals from one to ten are the basis of the number system. The numerals from eleven to nineteen are compounded of /arbəŋ/ 'ten' and the numerals one, two, three, etc.

The numerals from twenty to ninety are derived from the numerals two, three, etc., and display formative elements that are no longer productive.

There are special words for 100, 1000, 10,000, 100,000, and one million. The last two are borrowings from Tibetan.

The cardinal numerals from one to ten are:

1	/negə/	6	/ʒurgaaŋ/
2	/xoyər/	7	/dolooŋ/
3	/gurbəŋ/	8	/naeməŋ/
4	/dərbəŋ/	9	/yesəŋ/
5	/tabəŋ/	10	/arbəŋ/

The compound numerals from eleven to nineteen are:

11	/arbəŋ negə/	15	/arbəŋ tabəŋ/
12	/arbəŋ xoyər/	19	/arbəŋ yesəŋ/

The numerals from twenty to one hundred are:

20	/xoriŋ/	60	/ǰarəŋ/	100	/ʒuuŋ/
30	/gučiŋ/	70	/daləŋ/		
40	/dečiŋ/	80	/nayəŋ/		
50	/tabiŋ/	90	/yerəŋ/		

The numerals 21, 22, 23, etc., are composed of /xoriŋ/ and the numerals one, two, three, etc.

22	/xoriŋ xoyər/	45	/dečiŋ tabəŋ/
25	/xoriŋ Labəŋ/	56	/tabiŋ ʒurgaaŋ/
33	/gučiŋ gurbəŋ/	75	/daləŋ tabəŋ/

The numbers 200, 300, 400, etc., 2,000, 3,000, 4,000, etc., are composed of the numerals for 2, 3, 4, etc. and /ʒuuŋ/ 'hundred' or /miaŋgəŋ/ 'thousand', respectively.

200	/xoyər ʒuuŋ/		2,000	/xoyər miaŋgəŋ/
300	/gurbəŋ ʒuuŋ/		3,000	/gurbəŋ miaŋgəŋ/
500	/tabəŋ ʒuuŋ/		5,000	/tabəŋ miaŋgəŋ/

The numerals 10,000, 100,000, etc., use special words of foreign origin, as follows:

10,000 /tuməŋ/ (borrowed from Ancient Turkic)

100,000 /buməŋ/ (borrowed, like all the following numerals, from Tibetan)

1,000,000 /sayə/

10,000,000 /ǰibaa/

100,000,000 /dunčuur/

Instead of /tuməŋ/ and the other words for higher numbers, compound numerals may be used:

10,000   /arbəŋ miaŋgəŋ/

100,000   /ʒuuŋ miaŋgəŋ/

10,000,000   /arbəŋ sayə/

100,000,000   /ʒuuŋ sayə/

When functioning as nouns or adverbs, the numerals ending in /ŋ/ drop the /ŋ/, e.g. /gurbə/ 'three' (answering the question "How many are they?"); /gurbə irsəŋ/ 'came three times'. When functioning as adjectives (i.e. attributively), they retain the /ŋ/, e.g. /gurbəŋ xɯŋ/ 'three persons'.

3.24. Pronouns
Pronouns display special inflectional features (see 3.42).

3.25. Adverbs
The adverbs are a mixed class and include words that can be classified as defective nouns because most of them take only a few declension suffixes or represent petrified forms of nouns. Many of them take the reflexive-possessive suffix and occur with possessive forms of personal pronouns.

(1) Adverbs taking only the ablative suffix /+ees/ are: /endə/ 'here', /tendə/ 'there', /gadnə/ 'outside', /naanə/ 'on this side', /caanə/ 'on that side', /xaanə/ 'where?', /xoenə/ 'behind', /emnə/ 'in front of', etc.; cf. /endees/ 'from here', /gadnaas/ 'from without', /caanaas/ 'from the farther side'.

(2) Those taking only the dative-locative suffix /+də/ are: /caaši/ 'in that direction', /ɯrgəlji/ 'permanently, always', /gentə/ 'suddenly', /maši/ 'very much, greatly', etc.; cf. /caašidə/ 'in the future, since now', /ɯrgəljidə/ 'all the time', etc.

(3) Those taking the genitive suffix /+iiŋ/ are: /sayə/ 'just now, recently', cf. /sayəiiŋ/ 'of not long ago, recent'; /margaaši/ 'tomorrow', cf. /margaašiiŋ/ 'of tomorrow'; /ecəgdər/ 'yesterday', cf. /ecəgdəriiŋ/ 'of yesterday'; /negeedər/ 'the day after tomorrow', cf. /negeedəriiŋ/ 'of the day after tomorrow'.

(4) Those taking more than one case suffix are: /xeʒee/ (stem /xeʒeen+/) 'when?', cf. /xeʒeenees/ 'since when?', /xeʒeenii/ 'of long ago, ancient', /xeʒeedə/ 'always'; /gentə/ 'suddenly', cf. /gentədə/ 'suddenly', /gentəiiŋ/ 'of a sudden, sudden, unexpected'.

(5) The following invariable words can also be listed among the adverbs: /toŋ/ 'very, completely', cf. /toŋ buruu/ 'absolutely wrong'; /xaayaa/ 'sometimes'; /bas/ 'also, again'; /yaləŋguiyaa/ 'particularly' < Script Mongolian; /yaməgtə/ 'always' < Script Mongolian; /xugə/ 'asunder'; /xagə/ 'in two', cf. /xagə cabčibə/ 'he chopped [it] in two'; /tasə/ 'asunder'; /sugə/ 'out', cf. /sugə tatəbə/ 'he pulled it out'.

3.251. Demonstrative adverbs are: /endə/ 'here', /iiši/ 'hither', /enətee/ 'on this side', /tendə/ 'there', /tiiši/ 'in that direction', /tertee/ 'on that side', /naaši/ or /naeši/ 'in this direction', /caaši/ or /caeši/ 'in that direction', /ʉʉnčiləŋ/ 'in this way, thus', from /ʉʉn+/, stem of /enə/ 'this', /tʉʉnčiləŋ/ 'in that manner, thus, so', from /tʉʉn+/, stem of /terə/ 'that'.

3.252. Interrogative adverbs are /xeʒee/ 'when?', /xaa/ 'where?', /xaanə/ 'where?', /xaaši/ or /xaeši/ 'where to?'.

3.253. The emphasizing adverbs are /maši/ or /mašidə/ 'very much, greatly', cf. /maši saeŋ/ 'very good'; /neŋ/ 'very', cf. /nəŋ saeŋ/ 'very good'; /dendʉʉ/ 'too, more than enough', cf. /dendʉʉ oləŋ/ 'too many'; /daanč/ 'much too', cf. /daanč ertə/ 'much too early'.

3.254. Emphasizing adverbs, used with words denoting colors and a few other words, are formed with a reduplicating particle (C)Vb, in which C = the initial consonant (if any) of the word involved, and V = the first vowel, e.g. /xab xarə/ 'pitch-black',

/cab cagaaŋ/ 'snow-white', /ub ulaaŋ/ 'completely red', /geb gentə/ 'all of a sudden'.

3.26. Postpositions

The postpositions are a mixed category. Their functions are the same as those of English prepositions, with the difference that postpositions follow the words governed whereas prepositions precede them, e.g. /aǰiləiiŋ tul/ 'because of work' : /aǰil/ 'work', /tul/ 'because of'.

3.261. The genuine postpositions function only as postpositions. They do not occur freely and are invariable. The following postpositions belong to this category: /tul/ or /tuldə/ 'because of', with the genitive; /teləə/ 'instead of', with the genitive; /šaxəm/ or /šaxuu/ 'almost', with the subj.-obj. case, e.g. /arbə šaxuu/ 'almost ten'; /garui/ 'more than, exceeding', with the subj.-obj. case, e.g. /xori garui/ 'more than twenty'.

3.262. Some nouns, adverbs, and verbs may act as postpositions.

3.2621. Some postpositions are of nominal origin, e.g. /xaǰuudə/ 'at, by', from /xaǰuu/ 'side', e.g. /geriiŋ xaǰuudə/ 'by the house'; /xaǰuugaar/ 'along', instrumental of /xaǰuu/, e.g. /geriiŋ xaǰuugaar/ 'along the house'; /ačaar/ 'thanks to', in-strumental of /ači/ 'merit', e.g. /saeŋ emčiiŋ ačaar/ 'thanks to a good physician'; /učraas/ 'for the reason of, in conse-quence of', ablative of /učir/ 'reason, occasion', e.g. /əbčinii učraas/ 'because of illness'.

3.2622. Some postpositions are of adverbial origin, e.g. /naanə/ 'on this side', /goləiiŋ naanə/ 'on this side of the river', cf. /naanə baenə/ 'it is on this side'; /deerə/ 'above', /šireeŋ deerə/ 'on the table', cf. /deerə baenə/ 'it is above'; /dorə/ 'below, underneath', /geriiŋ dorə/ 'under the house', cf. /dorə baenə/ 'it is below'; /dergedə/ 'by the side', /geriiŋ dergədə/

'by the side of the house', cf. /dergədə baenə/ 'it is by the side'.

3.2623. Some postpositions are verbs, or, more precisely, gerunds, e.g. /xɯrtəl/ 'until, till', gerund of /xɯr-/ 'to reach, to arrive', e.g. /odoo xɯrtəl/ 'until now'; /exləŋ/ 'since, starting from', gerund of /exlə-/ 'to begin, to start', e.g. /bagə nasnaas exləŋ/ 'since childhood', lit. 'beginning from an early age'.

3.27 Verbs

The verbs have verbal inflection and serve, in their finite forms, as centers of verbal phrases. The verbal forms include the imperative, the tenses, verbal nouns, and gerunds, which are adverbs of verbal origin. The verbal nouns function as nouns (as syntactic subjects or complements), as adjectives (as syntactic attributes), and as finite verbs (syntactic predicates). The gerunds function as verbal attributes or adverbs.

3.271. The demonstrative verbs are /eŋgə-/ or /iŋgə-/ 'to act in this way', and /tegə-/ or /čiŋgə-/ 'to act in that way'. The gerunds of these verbs function as demonstrative adverbs, e.g. /iŋgəǰi/ 'acting in this way' = 'so'; /iŋgeed/ 'having acted in this way' = 'so, thus'; /tegəǰi/ 'acting in that way' = 'so'; /tegeed/ 'having acted in that way' = 'then'.

3.272. The interrogative verbs are /yaa-/ 'to do what?, to act how?' and /xaeči-/ 'to go where?'.

The gerunds of these verbs function as interrogative adverbs, e.g. /yaaǰi/ 'doing what?' = 'how?'; /yaagaad/ 'after having done what?' = 'why?'; /xaečiǰi yabaa/ 'where do you go?', lit. 'where going do you go?'.

3.28. Conjunctions

The conjunctions are invariable and are used to connect or to introduce clauses.

3.281. Co-ordinating conjunctions are the following:

(1) /ba/ 'and', which is used to connect words, e.g. /mal ba xədəə ajəxui/ 'cattle and rural economy'.

(2) /bəgəəd/ 'and', which is used to connect words and clauses, e.g. /sergələŋ bəgəəd gabšigae/ 'vigilant and dexterous'; /negəniini tolgoe cagaaŋ bəgəəd saxəlni xar/ 'the head of one of them was white and the beard was black'.

(3) /boləŋ/ 'and', which is used to connect words, e.g. /wilədbər boləŋ xedəlmərčid/ 'industry and the workers'.

In everyday speech these conjunctions are little used. Instead, numerals denoting the number of objects enumerated are used after the last word, e.g. /əbəgəŋ emgəŋ xoyər/ 'an old man and an old woman', lit. 'old man, old woman, two'; /xoni yamaa noxoe gurbə/ 'a sheep, a goat, and a dog', lit. 'sheep, goat, dog, three'.

(4) /buyuu/ 'or', e.g. /mod buyuu čuluu/ 'wood or stone'.

(5) /xariŋ/ 'but', e.g. /aduu baenə gesəŋ xariŋ wxər baebə/ '[he thought] it was a herd of horses, but it was a herd of oxen'.

(6) /esəbees/ or /esəbəl/ 'otherwise, or else', e.g. /či wldə esəbəl bi xamtə yabəyaa/ 'stay here, otherwise I shall go together with you'.

3.282. The subordinating conjunctions are the following:

(1) /gebəč/ 'although, however, and yet', e.g. /batəlsəŋ gebəč sergiilxə xerəgtee/ 'although he has fortified [it], nevertheless, it is necessary to be cautious'.

(2) /xerəb/ or /xerbee/ 'if', e.g. /xerbee či manaedə irəbəl/ 'if you come to us'.

3.29. Particles

The particles are invariable. They include the interrogative particles; negative, connecting, and confirmative particles; particles of probability; and adverbial particles.

3.291. The interrogative particles are /ɯɯ/, /šɯɯ/, and /bə/.

(1) The particle /ɯɯ/ ~ /yɯɯ/ complies with the rules of vowel harmony, and is /uu/ ~ /yuu/ with words with back vowels. It behaves like a suffix, but is not counted among the suffixes because it is neither a word-forming nor an inflectional element.

/ɯɯ/ and /uu/ are added to words ending in a consonant or in /ə/, e.g. /ta ɯʐəsənɯɯ/ 'have you seen?'; /enɯɯ/ < /enə+ɯɯ/ 'this?'.

/yɯɯ/ and /yuu/ are used after geminate vowel phonemes, diphthongs, and after single vowel phonemes of a monosyllable, e.g. /baenuu ɯgɯiyɯɯ/ 'is it or is it not?'; /gaxae yuu/ 'a pig?'; /ʐɯgeer ǰiriiŋ čimee yɯɯ/ 'just an ordinary rumor?'; /ta yuu/ 'you?'; /bi yɯɯ/ 'I?'.

(2) The particle /šɯɯ/ is a negative interrogative particle corresponding to French n'est-ce pas?. It is used in rhetorical questions, e.g. /bi yabəlaa šɯɯ/ 'I went, didn't I?'.

(3) The particle /bə/ or /b/, in emphatic speech /bee/, is added to the predicate of a clause which contains an interrogative word such as /xeŋ/ 'who?', /yamər/ 'what kind of?', /xaanə/ 'where?', /xeʐee/ 'when?', etc.; e.g. /ta yuu xiiǰ baenəb/ 'what are you doing?'; /xeŋ irsəŋbə/ 'who has come?'; /či xaečiǰ yabaa bee/ 'where are you going?'.

3.292. The negative particles are /gɯi/, /es/, /ɯl/, /bɯɯ/, /bitəgii/, /biši/, and /dɯi/.

(1) /gɯi/ goes back to the negative noun /ɯgɯi/ (cf. 3.211). It is attached to the end of nouns and all words functioning as nouns, including verbal nouns which, together with this particle, function as negative finite forms. The particle /gɯi/ does not comply with the rules of vowel harmony, e.g. /modəgɯi gaʐər/ 'a treeless country'; /irsəŋgɯi/ 'he has not come'.

(2) /es/ is a borrowing from Script Mongolian. It is used with verbal forms, except the imperative forms. It precedes the verbal form and corresponds in meaning to English not, e.g.

/es gɯicəbə/ 'he did not overtake'; /es medəbəl/ 'if he does not know'; /es medəǰi/ 'not knowing, unknowingly'.

(3) /ɯl/ is likewise a borrowing from Script Mongolian. It is used with verbal forms, except the imperative forms, and precedes the verbal form in question, e.g. /ɯl medəgči/ 'he who does not know', lit. 'not knowing one'; /ɯl xədəlxə xərəŋgə/ 'immovables', lit. 'property which does not move'; /ɯl bolnə/ 'is not permitted'.

(4) /bɯɯ/ is also a borrowing from Script Mongolian. It is a prohibitive particle and is used preceding the imperative forms of the verb. It corresponds in meaning to English <u>don't</u>, e.g. /bɯɯ xel/ 'don't say!'; /aebəl bɯɯ xii, xiibəl bɯɯ ae/ 'if you are afraid, don't do it; if you do it, don't be afraid!'.

(5) /bitəgii/ is a prohibitive particle and is used preceding the imperative forms of the verb. It corresponds to English <u>don't</u>, e.g. /bitəgii yabə/ 'don't go!'; /ta bitəgii yaaraarae/ 'you should not hurry!', lit. 'don't hurry!'.

(6) /biš/ or /biši/ negates the preceding and implies the opposite, i.e. it is translated as 'not... but...', e.g. /gišɯɯŋ biš/ 'not a member' (implies that he is an outsider); /enə minii nom biš/ 'this is not my book' (implies that it is someone else's book); /ta minii aǰil xiiǰi baegaa biš ulsəiiŋ aǰil xiiǰi baenə/ 'you do not work for me, but for the nation', lit. 'you are not doing my work, you are doing the work of the nation'.

(7) /dɯi/ 'not yet' is added to verbal nouns, usually to the verbal noun of the imperfect in /-ee/, e.g. /ireedɯi/ 'has not come yet'; /bidə yabəxədɯi/ 'we are not yet going'.

3.293. The particle /č/ is a connective-concessive particle. It is /č/ after a final vowel, and /či/ after a final consonant. It conveys the meanings 'and, also, too' and 'even', e.g. /bič medənə/ 'I, too, know [about it]'; /bi bodəsənčigɯi/ 'I have not even thought [about it]'; /terəč yabənə/ 'he, too, will go'.

3.294. The confirmative and emphasizing particles are /dee/, /l/, and /xөө/.

(1) /dee/ complies with the vowel harmony. It emphasizes a statement, e.g. /bagši irnə dee/ 'the teacher will, of course, come'; /bi tanaedə oči̯nə doo/ 'I shall by all means go to you'.

(2) /l/ is an emphasizing particle. Added to some verbal forms, it conveys the significance of 'still', e.g. /durtael baenə/ 'he really likes it'; /xecɯɯl xɯŋ šɯɯ/ 'a certainly difficult person, isn't he?'; /boroo orǰil baenə/ 'it is still raining'.

The particles /l/ and /dee/ are often used together, in order to further emphasize the statement, e.g. /togləyool doo/ 'let us play!', /өgəl dөө/ 'give it!'.

(3) The particle /xөө/ conveys the meaning 'exactly' and occurs mainly in poetry and folk songs, e.g. /ceŋxərləŋxəŋ xarəgdənə xөө/ 'it is seen light blue'.

3.210. Interjections

The interjections express sounds and noises. They occur mainly in preverbal position and are usually linked to other words by means of the verb /ge-/ 'to say', e.g. /xur xur/ sound of snoring; /tii tii yaasəŋ xaluuŋ yumbee/ 'whew, how hot it is!'; /usəndə cɯl getəl unəxə/ 'to fall into water so that it makes [the sound] tsul'; /xoŋ xoŋ xiiǰ baebə/ '[the bell] rang', lit. 'it was making [the sound] khon khon'.

3.3. Derivation

Word-formation or, more precisely, derivation of secondary stems from primary stems (or tertiary stems from secondary stems, etc.) is carried out by adding derivational suffixes to the stem concerned. In this manner, nouns are derived from nouns or verbs, and adverbs are derived from nouns, or verbs are derived from nouns, verbs, or interjections.

The derivational suffixes are attached to the stems, no other changes occurring in the latter except that stem-final

/n/ and a few other consonants at the end of a noun stem are
dropped before a derivational suffix.

Derivation by means of suffixes is the usual way of forming
words from other words, but it is not the only way, since words
can also be formed by compounding.

3.31. Nouns

Nouns can be formed from nouns, adjectives, numerals, and verbs.
Some suffixes of noun derivation also form adjectives. As a
general rule, stem-final /n/ of a primary noun is dropped before
a derivational suffix.

3.311. Nouns from nouns and adjectives

Nouns formed from nouns and adjectives may be divided into the
following semantic groups: names of professions, names of protective coverings, abstract nouns, diminutive nouns, collective
nouns, and names of plants and animals.

3.3111. Names of professions are formed with the suffixes /+či/
and /+čin+/.

(1) /+či/, e.g. /emči/ 'physician', from /em+/ 'medicine';
/altəči/ 'goldsmith', from /altən+/ 'gold'.

(2) /+čiŋ/, stem /+čin+/, e.g. /ajilčiŋ/ 'worker', from
/ajil+/ 'work'; /ɯildəbərčiŋ/ 'worker', from /ɯildəbər+/
'industry'.

3.3112. Names of protective coverings are formed with the suffix
/+bči/, e.g. /xuruubči/ 'thimble', from /xuruun+/ 'finger';
/xuʒuɯbči/ 'collar', from /xuʒuɯn+/ 'neck'; /salxibči/ 'cover
for an air vent', from /salxin+/ 'wind'.

3.3113. Abstract nouns are formed with the suffix /+ləg/, e.g.
/təmərləg/ 'metal', from /təmər+/ 'iron'; /bayələg/ 'wealth',
from /bayən+/ 'rich'; /niigəmləg/ 'society', from /niigəm+/
'society, community, common'.

3.3114. Diminutive nouns denote objects smaller in size than those
denoted by the primary noun stems; also various remote degrees
of kinship, e.g. "little grandson" = great-grandson. The suffix is /+ncər/, e.g. /uutəncər/ 'small bag', from /uutə+/ 'bag';
/čonəncər/ 'jackal', from /čonə+/ 'wolf'; /ɯnəgəncər/ 'raccoon',
from /ɯnəgən+/ 'fox'; /ʐeencər/ 'great-grandchild' (child of
Ego's daughter's child), from /ʐee+/ 'grandchild' (child of
Ego's daughter); /gučincər/ 'the son of Ego's great-great-
grandson', from /guči+/ 'great-great-grandson'.

3.3115. Collective nouns are formed with the suffixes /+čɯɯd/
(or /+čɯɯl/), and /+təŋ/.
    (1) /+čɯɯd/ or /+čɯɯl/, e.g. /bayəčuud/ or /bayəčuul/
'rich people, capitalists, bourgeoisie', from /bayən+/ 'rich';
/ʐaluučuud/ 'youth, young persons, youth league', from /ʐaluu+/
'young'; /idərčɯɯl/ 'youth', from /idər+/ 'young'.
    (2) /+təŋ/ (stem /+tən+/), e.g. /araatəŋ/ 'the class of
carnivorous animals', from /araan+/ 'molar tooth'; /tuuraetəŋ/
'the class of ungulate animals', from /tuurae+/ 'hoof';
/xərəŋgətəŋ/ 'bourgeoisie', from /xərəŋgə+/ 'property, capital';
/erdəmtəŋ/ 'scholars'; /ɯʐəltəŋ/ 'those who share a common view',
from /ɯʐəl+/ 'view, opinion'.
    Words ending in /+təŋ/ often have a singular meaning, e.g.
/oyuutəŋ/ 'student', from /oyuun+/ 'wisdom, intellect'; /amitəŋ/
'living being, animal', from /amin+/ 'life'; /mergəǰiltəŋ/
'specialist', from /mergəǰil+/ 'specialty, profession'.

3.3116. Names of plants and animals are formed with the suffixes
/+gənə/, /+lʐəgənə/, /+lʐae/, /+lǰi/, and /+dae/.
    (1) /+gənə/, e.g. /ulaagənə/ 'red currant', from /ulaan+/
'red'; /xargənə/ 'caragana' (a plant), from /xarə/ 'black';
/šɯɯdərgənə/ 'Chelidonium L.' (a plant), from /šɯɯdər+/ 'dew';
/xulgənə/ 'mouse', from /xulə+/ 'grey'; /xedəgənə/ 'bumblebee',
from /xedər+/ 'obstinate'.

(2) /+lƺəgənə/, e.g. /šarəlƺəgənə/ name of a plant, from /šarə+/ 'yellow'; /temeelƺəgənə/ 'dragonfly', from /temeen+/ 'camel'.

(3) /+lƺae/, e.g. /ulaalƺae/ 'lilium sarana' (a plant), from /ulaan+/ 'red'; /borəlƺoe/ name of a plant, from /borə+/ 'grey'.

(4) /+lǰi/, e.g. /šarəlǰi/ 'artemisia', from /šarə+/ 'yellow'; /borəlǰi/ a species of birch, from /borə+/ 'grey'; /ulaalǰi/ name of a plant, from /ulaan+/ 'red'; /naeməlǰi/ 'crab', from /naemən+/ 'eight'.

(5) /+dae/, e.g. /doloodoe/ 'Trientalis europea L.' (a plant), from /doloon+/ 'seven'; /ƺurgaadae/ name of a bush, from /ƺurgaan+/ 'six'.

3.3117. Nouns with various meanings are formed with the suffixes /+ləŋ/ and /+ldee/.

(1) /+ləŋ/ (stem /+ləŋg+/ before a suffix with a vowel at the onset), e.g. /tariaaləŋ/ 'field', from /tariaan+/ 'crops'; /xʉreeləŋ/ 'committee', from /xʉreen+/ 'circle, fence'; /duguiləŋ/ 'circle' (political, social), from /dugui+/ 'wheel, anything that is round'; /urəsxələŋ/ 'current' (of water), from /urəsxə/ 'streaming, running'; /šʉdləŋ/ an animal at the age when it changes its teeth, from /šʉdən+/ 'tooth'; /soyooləŋ/ an animal at the age when it grows new canine teeth, from /soyoon+/ 'canine tooth'.

(2) /+ldee/, e.g. /xʉʉxəldee/ 'doll', from /xʉʉxən+/ 'girl'; /booxəldoe/ 'devil', from /booxə+/ 'he who makes obstacles'.

3.312. <u>Nouns from numerals</u>

Nouns are formed from numerals with the suffixes /+uul/, /+lǰiŋ/, and /+dae/.

(1) /+uul/ (stem /+uulən+/), e.g. /xoyuul/ 'the two together', from /xoyər+/ 'two'; /gurbuul/ 'the three together', from /gurbən+/ 'three'.

90

(2) /+lǰiŋ/ (stem /+lǰin+/, forming names of geometrical figures, e.g. /gurbəlǰiŋ/ 'triangle, triangular', from /gurbən+/ 'three'; /dərbəlǰiŋ/ 'square', from /dərbən+/ 'four'; /tabəlǰiŋ/ 'pentagon, pentagonal', from /tabən+/ 'five'.

(3) /+dae/, see 3.3116.(5).

3.313. Nouns from verbs

Nouns from verbs are formed with a variety of suffixes. With a few exceptions, e.g. names of tools, most nouns derived from verbs cannot be assigned to any particular semantic group.

(1) /-ee/ (stem /-een+/) typically forms nouns denoting the process of an action, e.g. /barildaa/ 'wrestling', from /barildə-/ 'to wrestle'; /xeləlcee/ 'discussion, negotiations', from /xeləlcə-/ 'to discuss, to negotiate'; /xaraa/ 'eyesight', from /xarə-/ 'to look at something'.

(2) /-eeči/ (< /-ee/ + /+či/ [3.3111.(1)]), treated here as a separate suffix although it is a compound in origin because it is often found on verbal stems which do not form the verbal noun in /-ee/, forms agent nouns, e.g. /bičeeči/ 'scribe', from /biči-/ 'to write'; /ʒuraači/ 'painter', from /ʒurə-/ 'to paint, to draw'; /alaači/ 'killer, murderer', from /al-/ 'to kill'. (None of these verbs forms the verbal noun in /-ee/.)

(3) /-ɯɯl/ forms agent nouns, e.g. /xaruul/ 'sentry, sentinel', from /xarə-/ 'to look at something'; /turšuul/ 'scout', from /turši-/ 'to explore, to reconnoiter'; /daguul/ 'follower, companion', from /dagə-/ 'to follow'.

(4) /-ɯɯr/ forms names of tools (with stems containing the phoneme /r/, the suffix is /-ɯɯl/), e.g. /maltuur/ 'wooden shovel, snow shovel', from /maltə-/ 'to dig'; /əlgɯɯr/ 'hanger', from /əlgə-/ 'to hang up'; /bariuul/ 'handle', from /bari-/ 'to seize, to take'.

(5) /-ɯɯri/ (with stems containing the phoneme /r/, the suffix is /-ɯɯli/), e.g. /agnuuri/ 'hunting ground', from /agnə-/ 'to hunt'; /togtuuri/ 'stability, permanence', from /togtə-/ 'to become stable, to be stabilized'; /ʒobuuri/ 'suffering',

from /ʒobə-/ 'to suffer'; /surguuli/ 'school', from /surgə-/
'to teach'.

(6) /-ri/, e.g. /baeri/ 'quarters', from /bae-/ 'to be,
to stay'; /suuri/ 'basis, seat', from /suu-/ 'to sit down';
/xebtəri/ 'bed, anything to lie on', from /xebtə-/ 'to lie
down'; /neməri/ 'addition', from /nemə-/ 'to add'.

(7) /-eeŋ/ (stem /-een+/), e.g. /baeldaaŋ/ 'war', from
/baeldə-/ 'to fight'; /šʉteeŋ/ 'holy image, object of veneration
or worship', from /šʉtə-/ 'to believe in something'; /xubilgaaŋ/
'transformation, reincarnation of a saint, a reincarnated saint',
from /xubilgə-/ 'to transform'.

(8) /-m/, e.g. /xerčim/ 'piece', from /xerči-/ 'to cut';
/toxəm/ 'saddlecloth', from /toxə-/ 'to saddle'; /ʒʉsəm/ 'piece,
slice', from /ʒʉsə-/ 'to cut'.

(9) /-g/, e.g. /bičig/ 'letter', from /biči-/ 'to write';
/ʒurəg/ 'picture', from /ʒurə-/ 'to draw'; /ʒorig/ 'valiancy',
from /ʒori-/ 'to be determined'; /gunig/ 'sadness', from /guni-/
'to be sad'.

(10) /-ʒə/ typically forms nouns denoting the result of an
action, e.g. /olʒə/ 'booty, profit', from /ol-/ 'to find, to
obtain'; /garʒə/ 'expense', from /gar-/ 'to go out'; /orʒə/
'income', from /orə-/ 'to come in'.

(11) /-s/ (stem /-sən+/), e.g. /nulməs/ 'tear', from
/nulmə-/ 'to spit'; /xees/ 'foam', from /xee-/ 'to swell, to
rise' (dough).

(12) /-ees/ (stem /-eesən+/), e.g. /xadaas/ 'nail', from
/xadə-/ 'to drive in'; /nexees/ 'patch', from /nexə-/ 'to mend'.

(13) /-eer/, e.g. /belčeer/ 'grazing, pasture', from
/belči-/ 'to graze'; /ʉdeer/ 'a thin leather thong', from /ʉdə-/
'to sew'.

(14) /-məg/, e.g. /xuurməg/ 'fraud', from /xuur-/ 'to
deceive'; /xoliməg/ 'mixture', from /xoli-/ 'to mix'.

(15) /-š/ or /-ši/, e.g. /idəš/ 'food', from /idə-/ 'to
eat'; /buləš/ 'grave, tomb', from /bulə-/ 'to inter'; /tʉləš/
'fuel', from /tʉl-/ 'to burn'.

(16) /-li/, e.g. /saali/ 'yield of milk', from /saa-/ 'to milk'; /sacəli/ 'libation', from /sacə-/ 'to strew, to sprinkle'.

(17) /-l/, e.g. /ɯxəl/ 'death', from /ɯxə-/ 'to die'; /ǰargəl/ 'happiness', from /ǰargə-/ 'to be happy'.

(18) /-cə/, e.g. /ʒarcə/ 'servant', from /ʒarə-/ 'to employ someone'; /yabəcə/ 'process, course' (of an affair), from /yabə-/ 'to walk, to go'.

(19) /-mtə/, e.g. /barimtə/ 'fact' (originally, 'what one can seize, anything tangible'), from /bari-/ 'to seize, to take'; /boomtə/ 'roadblock, a border checkpoint', from /boo / 'to bind, to obstruct'.

(20) /-ltə/, e.g. /neməltə/ 'addition', from /nemə-/ 'to add'; /yaləltə/ 'victory', from /yalə-/ 'to conquer'; /booltə/ 'band, string, tire', from /boo-/ 'to bind'.

(21) /-lgə/ (stem /-lgən+/), e.g. /uŋšilgə/ 'reading', from /uŋši-/ 'to read'; /xaalgə/ 'gate', from /xaa-/ 'to close'.

(22) /-bər/, e.g. /taelbər/ 'commentary, explanation', from /tael-/ 'to explain'; /ɯildəbər/ 'industry', from /ɯiləd-/ 'to work, to do something'.

(23) /-mər/, e.g. /xədəlmər/ 'work', from /xədəl-/ 'to move, to work'.

(24) /-dəl/ (after stem-final /r/, the suffix is /-təl/), e.g. /baedəl/ 'situation', from /bae-/ 'to be'; /yabədəl/ 'action', from /yabə-/ 'to move, to go, to act'; /surtəl/ 'doctrine', from /sur-/ 'to learn, to study'.

(25) /-dəs/ (stem /-dəsən+/), e.g. /oroodəs/ 'wrapping', from /oroo-/ 'to wrap'; /ʒardəs/ 'woman servant', from /ʒarə-/ 'to employ'.

(26) /-mǰi/, e.g. /serəmǰi/ 'vigilance', from /serə-/ 'to stay awake, to be alert'; /texeerəmǰi/ 'equipment', from /texeer-/ 'to equip'.

(27) /-də/ (stem /-dən+/), e.g. /xaniaadə/ 'cough', from /xaniaa-/ 'to cough'; /ineedə/ 'laughter', from /inee-/ 'to laugh'.

(28) /-ləŋ/ (stem /-ləŋ+/), e.g. /ǰargələŋ/ 'happiness', from /ǰargə-/ 'to be happy'; /ʒobələŋ/ 'suffering', from /ʒobə-/ 'to suffer'; /xadələŋ/ 'meadow, hay field', from /xadə-/ 'to mow'.

(29) /-gə/, e.g. /taniuulgə/ 'information', from /taniuul-/ 'to make acquainted with something, to let know'; /orčuulgə/ 'translation', from /orčuul-/ 'to translate'.

(30) /-xuɯŋ/ (stem /-xuɯn+/), e.g. /buteegdəxuɯŋ/ 'production, product', from /buteegdə-/ 'to be produced'; /surtəxuuŋ/ 'morale', from /surtə-/ 'to be studied, to be learned'.

(31) /-sgələŋ/ (stem /-sgələŋ+/), e.g. /uʒəsgələŋ/ 'spectacle, exhibition', from /uʒə-/ 'to see'; /bayəsgələŋ/ 'joy', from /bayəs-/ 'to rejoice'.

(32) /-uɯrgə/ typically forms names of tools, e.g. /xešuɯrgə/ 'lever', from /xeši-/ 'to prop up'; /damnuurgə/ 'carrying-pole, yoke', from /damnə-/ 'to carry something by means of a yoke'.

(33) /-b/, e.g. /təsəb/ 'budget, estimate of cost', from /təsə-/ 'to conjecture, to make an estimate'; /sedəb/ 'subject, topic', from /sedə-/ 'to plan'.

3.314. Compound nouns

Compound nouns are formed either by co-ordinate or subordinate composition.

3.3141.

Compound nouns formed by co-ordinate composition are usually called "binoms". They consist of two nouns, neither of which is governed by the other. In writing they are rendered as two words, with the exception of proper names, e.g. personal names, names of cities, etc. The juncture between the two words is the compound juncture (see 2.13), e.g. /aduuməl/ 'cattle, domestic animals', from /aduu/ 'herd of horses' and /mal/ 'cattle'; /erdəmsoyəl/ 'education', from /erdəm/ 'wisdom, knowledge, science' and /soyəl/ 'culture'; /argəxemǰee/ 'measure' (applied in order to achieve something, e.g. drastic measures),

from /argə/ 'means' and /xemǰee/ 'size, measure' (such as length);
/gaʒərusə/ 'territory', from /gaʒər/ 'earth' and /usə/ 'water';
/orəlgəʒarəlgə/ 'budget', from /orəlgə/ 'income' and /ʒarəlgə/
'expense'; /lubsəndendəb/ the name of a person, from /lubsəŋ/
and /dendəb/.

3.3142. Compound nouns formed by subordinate composition are of
two types.

(1) The first member is comparable to an attribute. It
is either a noun functioning as an adjective, or an adjective,
or numeral, e.g. /gaʒərʒui/ 'geography', from /gaʒər/ 'earth'
and /ʒui/ 'rule'; /ulaambaatər/ 'the city of Ulaanbaatar', from
/ulaan/ 'red' and /baatər/ 'hero'; /šaršəbuu/ 'horned owl', from
/šar/ 'yellow' and /šubuu/ 'bird'; /nəgeedər/ 'the day after
tomorrow', from /nəgee/ 'next, second' and /edər/ 'day'.

Some compound nouns of this type are written together, others
are treated in the orthography as two words.

(2) The first member of the compound is comparable to a
direct object governed by the second member, e.g. /čuluubutəluur/
'rock crusher', from /čuluu/ 'rock, stone' and /butəluur/ 'break-
er, a crushing-machine'; /šoroodxuur/ 'dredger', from /šoroo/
'earth' and /udxuur/ 'scoop'.

3.32. Adjectives

All adjectives can be substantivized, i.e. function as nouns.
As such, they can take the plural suffix, occur in all case
forms, and take the possessive suffixes. Adjectives are derived
from nouns, adjectives, numerals, adverbs, and verbs.

3.321. Adjectives from nouns

Most nouns function as adjectives without any particular suffix,
e.g. /temər/ 'iron', which is a noun in the phrase /xatuu temər/
'hard iron', but an adjective in the phrase /temər xubiŋ/ 'iron
bucket'.

Nouns with stems ending in /n/ alternating with zero form adjectives with a final /ŋ/, e.g. /modə/, stem /modən+/ 'wood', but /modəŋ/ 'wooden'; /altə/, stem /altən+/ 'gold', but /altəŋ/ 'golden'; /čuluu/, stem /čuluun+/ 'stone, rock', but /čuluuŋ/ 'stone (adj.), of stone'; /us/, stem /usən+/ 'water', but /usəŋ/ 'pertaining to water, aquatic'.

Adjectives are also formed from nouns by means of suffixes.

(1) /+ləg/ typically forms adjectives denoting possession of a quality, e.g. /tosləg/ 'fat, oily', from /tos/ (stem /tosən+/) 'grease, fat, butter, oil'; /sɯrləg/ 'majestic, imposing, impressive', from /sɯr/ 'grandeur, greatness, majesty'; /šabərləg/ 'muddy, pertaining to clay', from /šabər/ 'clay, mud'; /usləg/ 'watery' from /us/ (stem /usən+/) 'water'.

(2) /+msəg/, e.g. /goyəmsəg/ 'dandy', from /goyə+/ 'elegance'; /yixəmsəg/ 'haughty', from /yixə/ 'greatness, great'; /torgəmsəg/ 'silky', from /torəg/ (stem /torgən+/) 'silk'.

(3) /+bxi/, e.g. /usəbxi/ 'watery', from /us/ (stem /usən+/) 'water'; /idəbxi/ 'active, energetic', from /idə/ 'energy, dexterity'.

(4) /+xii ~ +xae ~ +xoe/, e.g. /sɯrxii/ 'serious, terrific', from /sɯr/ 'grandeur, majesty'; /balərxae/ 'indistinct, obscure', from /balər/ 'darkness, gloom'; /xoŋxərxoe/ 'uneven' (road), from /xoŋxər/ 'hole' (in the ground, road, etc.); /nabtərxae/ 'ragged', from /nabtəs/ (stem /nabtəsən+/) 'rags'.

(5) /+də/, e.g. /amidə/ 'live, living', from /amin+/ 'life'; /dornədə/ 'eastern', from /dornə+/ 'east'.

(6) /+tə/ forms adjectives denoting possession of something, e.g. /albətə/ 'subject', from /albən+/ 'corvée, service'; /čuluutə/ 'stony', from /čuluun+/ 'stone'.

Adjectives ending in /+tə/ very often function as substantives, and many place names in Mongolia are adjectives in origin, e.g. /erdəmtə/ 'scholar, savant', from /erdəm+/ 'science'; /galuutə/ 'abounding in geese' (a place name), from /galuun+/ 'goose'.

(7) /+tee ~ +tae ~ +toe/ forms adjectives denoting possession of something, e.g. /uxaantae/ 'intelligent', from
/uxaan+/ 'intellect'; /moritoe/ 'having a horse', from /morin+/
'horse'; /galtae/ 'fiery', from /gal+/ 'fire'; /gertee/ or
/gertei/ 'married, possessing a home of his own', from /ger+/
'house, home'.

3.322. Adjectives from adjectives

Adjectives formed from adjectives include the diminutive and
feminine forms.

3.3221. The diminutive adjectives are mainly formed from color
names and denote weak shades of colors. Only the suffix /+xəŋ/
is taken by all adjectives, or nouns functioning as adjectives.

(1) /+xəŋ/ (stem /+xən+/) forms adjectives of endearment,
i.e. adjectives denoting various qualities of persons, animals,
etc., that are spoken of affectionately, e.g. /ulaaŋxəŋ cecəg/
'a red floweret', from /ulaan+/ 'red'; /xetəxəŋ gaʒər/ '[your]
distant [dear] homeland', from /xetə+/ 'distant'; /goyəxəŋ/
'pretty', from /goyə/ 'elegance, elegant'.

The suffix /+xəŋ/, although added to an adjective, often
refers to the following noun, e.g. /xarəxəŋ mori/ 'little black
horse' (cf. 'horsey' in nursery talk), and not 'a rather black
horse'.

The suffix /+xəŋ/ is also taken by numerals, and forms
diminutive numerals, e.g. /gurbəŋxəŋ/ 'only three', from
/gurbən+/ 'three'; /arbəŋxəŋ/ 'only ten', from /arbən+/ 'ten'.

In sagas, the suffix /+xəŋ/ is also taken by the gerund in
/-ŋ/ when it refers to persons spoken of affectionately, e.g.
/eʒələŋxəŋ tərəsəŋ/ 'born to rule', from /eʒələŋ/ 'ruling',
from /eʒəl-/ 'to rule'.

(2) /+btər/ forms names of weak shades of color and other
weak qualities, e.g. /ulaabtər/ 'reddish', from /ulaan+/ 'red';
/xarəbtər/ 'blackish', from /xarə+/ 'black'; /yaduubtər/ 'rather

poor', from /yaduu+/ 'poor'; /xeltəgiibtər/ 'somewhat awry', from /xeltəgii+/ 'awry, oblique'.

(3) /+ŋgui/ forms names of weak shades of colors, e.g. /borəŋgui/ 'rather grey, greyish', from /borə+/ 'grey'; /šarəŋgui/ 'rather yellow, yellowish', from /šarə+/ 'yellow'.

(4) /+dɯɯ/ forms names of weak shades of colors, e.g. /xəxədɯɯ/ 'bluish', from /xəxə+/ 'blue'.

(5) /+mdəg/, e.g. /xəxəmdəg/ 'bluish', from /xəxə+/ 'blue'.

3.3222. Mongolian has no grammatical gender, and the form of an adjective is the same whether it refers to a male or female person, with the exception of adjectives which denote the age or color of domestic animals.

(1) /+gčiŋ/ (stem /+gčin+/) forms adjectives denoting colors of female domestic animals, e.g. /xarəgčiŋ ɯnee/ 'black cow' (cf. /xarə buxə+/ 'black bull'); /cagaagčiŋ gɯɯ/ 'white mare' (cf. /cagaaŋ aʒərgə+/ 'white stallion').

When substantivized, these forms drop their final /ŋ/, e.g. /xarəgči/ 'the black one, Blackie', /cagaagči/ 'the white one, Whitey'.

(2) /+ǰiŋ/ (stem /+ǰin+/) forms adjectives denoting the age of female animals, e.g. /gunəǰiŋ ɯnee/ 'a three-year-old cow' (cf. /gunəŋ buxə/ 'a three-year-old bull'); /dənəǰiŋ temee/ 'a three-year-old female camel' (cf. /dənəŋ temee/ 'a three-year-old male camel').

When substantivized, these forms drop their final /ŋ/, e.g. /gunəǰi/ 'the three-year-old one'.

3.323. <u>Adjectives from numerals</u>

Adjectives formed from numerals comprise ordinal numerals, distributive numerals, diminutive numerals, and adjectives denoting age.

3.3231. The ordinal numerals are formed with the suffixes /+dɯgeer/ and /+dəxi/.

(1) /+dɯgeer/, borrowed from Script Mongolian, has the allomorphs /+dɯgeer/ on stems with front vowels, and /+dugaar/ on stems with back vowels, e.g. /negədɯgeer/ 'first', from /negə/ (stem /negən+/) 'one'; /xoyərdugaar/ 'second', from /xoyər+/ 'two'; /arbədugaar/ 'tenth', from /arbəŋ/ (stem /arbən+/) 'ten'.

It is also taken by the interrogative adjective /xedəŋ/ (stem /xedən+/) 'how many?'.

(2) /+dəxi/ forms ordinal numerals, e.g. /negədəxi/ 'first', from /negə/ (stem /negən+/) 'one'; /gurbədəxi/ 'third', from /gurbəŋ/ (stem /gurbən+/) 'three'.

3.3232. The distributive and approximative numerals are formed with the suffix /+eed/ 'by twos, each two, two (to each one)', 'by threes, each three, three (to each one)', etc. The numbers one and two have irregular forms. The other meaning of such numerals is "approximately so and so many", e.g. /nejeed/ 'by ones, each one, one (to each one)', from /negə/ 'one'; /xošood/ 'by twos, each two, two (to each one)', from /xoyər+/ 'two'; /gurbaad/ 'by threes, each three, three (to each one), approximately three', from /gurbən+/ 'three'; /xoriood/ 'by twenties, each twenty, twenty (to each one), approximately twenty', from /xorin+/ 'twenty'; /ʒuugaad/ 'by hundreds, each hundred, hundred (to each one), approximately a hundred', from /ʒuun+/ 'hundred'.

3.3233. The diminutive numerals ("only three", "only five", etc.) are formed with the suffix /+xeŋ/, see 3.3221.(1).

3.3234. Adjectives denoting age are formed with the suffix /+tee/, see 3.321.(7), e.g. /gurbətae/ 'three-year-old', from /gurbən+/ 'three'; /arbətae/ 'ten-year-old', from /arbən+/ 'ten'; /xorin+tabətae/ 'twenty-five-year-old', from /xorin+tabən+/ 'twenty-five'.

3.324. <u>Adjectives from adverbs</u>

Adjectives are formed from adverbs with the suffixes /+də/ and
/+xi/.

(1) /+də/, see 3.321.(5), e.g. /gadaadə/ 'outer', from
/gadaa+/ 'out, without'; /caadə/ 'remote, that on the farther
side of something', from /caa+/, in /caaši/ 'in that direction'.

(2) /+xi/ with adverbs of place, the dative-locative and
genitive of nouns, and the genitive of the personal pronouns,
e.g. /endəxi/ 'of this place', from /endə/ 'here'; /xoešixi/
'hind, back', from /xoeši/ 'backwards'; /deeguɯrxi/ 'upper',
from /deeguɯr/ 'above, along the top'; /gertəxi/ 'domestic',
from /gertə/ 'in the house' (dat.-loc.), from /ger+/ 'yurt,
house'; /usəndəxi/ 'aquatic', from /usəndə/ 'in the water'
(dat.-loc.), from /usən+/ 'water'; /xaanaexi/ 'khan's, that of
the khan, royal', from /xaanae/ 'of the khan' (gen.), from
/xaan+/ 'khan, king'; /axəiiŋxi/ 'that of the elder brother',
from /axəiiŋ/ 'of the elder brother', from /axə+/ 'elder
brother'; /manaexi/ 'ours', from /manae/ 'of us', gen. of
/bidə/ 'we'.

3.325. <u>Adjectives from verbs</u>

Adjectives from verbs are formed with the suffixes /-uɯ/,
/-uɯŋ/, /-gii/, /-gər/, /-mxii/, /-mtəgii/, /-ŋgi/, /-ŋxii/,
/-ee/, /-uɯr/, /-š+guɯ/.

(1) /-uɯ/, e.g. /xatuu/ 'hard', from /xatə-/ 'to dry up,
to harden'; /sogtuu/ 'drunk, intoxicated', from /sogtə-/ 'to
become drunk'.

(2) /-uɯŋ/, e.g. /ernuɯŋ/ 'developed', from /ernə-/ 'to
develop'; /xaluuŋ/ 'hot', from /xal-/ 'to become hot'.

(3) /-gii/, replacing final /ii/ of the stem, and
/-gae ~ -goe/, replacing final /ae oe/, respectively, e.g.
/xeltəgii/ 'slanting', from /xeltii-/ 'to slant'; /xaʒəgae/
'awry, oblique', from /xaʒae-/ 'to be awry'.

(3) /-gər/ replacing final /ii ae oe/ of the stem, e.g.
/sertəgər/ 'standing on edge, bristling', from /sertii-/ 'to

100

bristle'; /gialgər/ 'shining, glittering', from /gialae-/ 'to shine, to glitter'; /xotᵊgər/ 'concave, hollow', from /xotoe-/ 'to be bent, to bend in'.

(5) /-mxii ∼ -mxae ∼ -mxoe/, e.g. /idəmxii/ 'ravenous, avaricious', from /idə-/ 'to eat'; /aemxae/ 'timid, fearful', from /ae-/ 'to be afraid'; /orəmxoe/ 'having access to something, having the permission to enter a place at any given time', from /orə-/ 'to enter'.

(6) /-mtəgii ∼ -mtəgae ∼ -mtəgoe/, e.g. /aemtəgae/ 'timid, fearful', from /ae-/ 'to be afraid; /ičimtᵊgii/ 'shy, bashful', from /iči-/ 'to be ashamed'; /orəmtəgoe/ 'having access to something, having the permission to go in at any time', from /orə-/ 'to enter'.

(7) /-ŋgi ∼ -ŋgə/, e.g. /xatəŋgi/ 'lean', from /xatə-/ 'to dry up'; /yadəŋgi/ 'poor', from /yadə-/ 'to be poor, to be unable'; /xatəŋgə/ 'strong, hard', from /xatə-/ 'to harden'; /seeŋgə/ 'hoarse', from /see-/ 'to be hoarse'.

(8) /-ŋxii/, e.g. /ecəŋxii/ 'lean', from /ecə-/ 'to be exhausted'; /turəŋxae/ 'lean', from /turə-/ 'to become lean, to lose weight'.

(9) /-ee/, e.g. /guŋšaa/ 'having a nasal twang', from /guŋši-/ 'to speak through the nose'; /goŋginoo/ 'whimpering', from /goŋginə-/ 'to whimper'.

(10) /-ɯɯr/, see 3.313.(4), e.g. /xianuur/ 'careful, observant, alert', from /xianə-/ 'to keep under observation'; /nialgənuur/ 'sticky', from /nialgənə-/ 'to be sticky, to stick to something'.

(11) /-š+gɯi/, composed of /-š/, see 3.313.(15), and the negative particle /gɯi/, see 3.292.(1), forms adjectives denoting unfitness, e.g. /uuš+gɯi/ 'undrinkable', from /uu-/ 'to drink'; /xeləš+gɯi/ 'unspeakable, inexpressible', from /xelə-/ 'to say, to speak'; /ɯʒəš+gɯi/ 'ugly, disgusting, nothing to look at', from /ɯʒə-/ 'to see'.

3.326. Compound adjectives

Compound adjectives are composed of two adjectives, or of a
noun and an adjective. The compounds are of two types, co-
ordinate and subordinate.

3.3261. Co-ordinate compounds are composed of two adjectives,
e.g. /aguuyixə/ 'enormous', from /aguu/ 'vast' and /yixə/
'large'; /šarəlaaŋ/ 'yellowish-red', from /šar/ 'yellow' and
/ulaaŋ/ 'red'; /xarbəraaŋ/ 'dark colored', from /xar/ 'black'
and /baraaŋ/ 'dark'; /xarxɯrəŋ/ 'dark brown', from /xar/
'black' and /xɯrəŋ/ 'brown'.

3.3262. Subordinate compounds are composed of two adjectives, or
of a noun and an adjective.

   (1) The first adjective denotes a quality with which that
of the second adjective is compared, e.g. /casəncəgaaŋ/ 'snow-
white', from /casəŋ/ 'snowy, pertaining to snow, of snow' and
/cagaaŋ/ 'white'; /cusənəlaaŋ/ 'blood-red, red as blood', from
/cusəŋ/ 'bloody, pertaining to blood' and /ulaaŋ/ 'red';
/altənšər/ 'yellow as gold', from /altəŋ/ 'golden' and /šar/
'yellow'.

   (2) The second adjective is formed with the suffix
/+tee ~ +tae ~ +toe/, see 3.321.(7), and the first adjective is
an attribute of the second adjective, e.g. /šardeeltee/ 'yellow-
robed', from /šar/ 'yellow' and /deeltee/ 'having a robe';
/urtəčixitee/ 'long-eared', from /urtə/ 'long' and /čixitee/
'having ears'; /morinǰiltee/ 'born in the year of the horse',
from /moriŋ/ 'equine' and /ǰiltee/ 'having the year of'.

   (3) A special case is a compound composed of a numeral
adjective and another adjective, e.g. /dərbəŋxəltee/ 'four-
legged', from /dərbəŋ/ 'four' and /xəltee/ 'having legs';
/tabəŋxəšuutae od/ 'a five-pointed star', from /tabəŋ/ 'five'
and /xošuutae/ 'having points', from /xošuun+/ 'point'.

   (4) The first member is a noun, and the second member is
an adjective ending in /+tee ~ +tae ~ +toe/, e.g. /morisaetae/

'having good horses', from /mori/ 'horse' and /saetae/ 'having
something good', from /saeŋ/ 'good'; /čanərsaetae/ 'of good
quality', from /čanər/ 'quality' and /saeĿae/ 'having something
good'; /šɯdəmuutae/ 'having bad teeth', from /šɯdə/ 'tooth,
teeth' and /mɯutae/ 'having something bad', from /muu/ 'bad';
/usyixətee/ 'having much water, abounding in water, well-
irrigated', from /us/ 'water' and /yixətee/ 'having something
big', from /yixə/ 'big, large, much'.

3.33. Adverbs

Adverbs are formed from nouns, adjectives, numerals, adverbs,
and verbs.

3.331. Adverbs from nouns

Adverbs from nouns are formed with the suffixes /+cee/, /+ǰiŋ/,
/+də/, and /+gɯɯr/.

(1) /+cee/ forms adverbs denoting the height reached by
something, e.g. /əbədəgcөө/ 'up to the knees', from /əbədəg/
'knee'.

(2) /+ǰiŋ/ forms adverbs denoting the length of time,
e.g. /ədərǰiŋ/ 'the whole day', from /ədər/ 'day'.

(3) /+də/, with final /n/ of the stem dropped, e.g.
/nasədə/ 'always', from /nas/ (stem /nasən+/) 'lifetime'.

(4) /+gɯɯr/, e.g. /əgleегɯɯr/ 'in the morning', from
/əglee/ 'morning'; /oroeguur/ 'in the evening', from /oroe/
'evening'.

3.332. Adverbs from adjectives

Adverbs from adjectives are formed with the suffixes /+də/,
/+tər/, /+eeši/, and /+ɯɯr/.

(1) /+də/, e.g. /yixədə/ 'greatly', from /yixə/ 'great,
large'; /ɯrgəlǰidə/ 'always, continuously', from /ɯrgəlǰi/
'permanent'.

(2) /+tər/, with the stem-final /n/ dropped, e.g. /saetər/
'well', from /saeŋ/ (stem /saen+/) 'good'.

(3) /+eeši/, e.g. /urtaaši/ 'lengthwise', from /urtə/ 'long'.

(4) /+ɯɯr/, e.g. /xoluur/ 'far away', from /xolə/ 'far, distant'; /urduur/ 'along the front side', from /urdə/ 'front, frontal'.

3.333. Adverbs from numerals

Adverbs from numerals are formed with the suffix /+tə/. These are the so-called multiplicative numerals, e.g. /negəntə/ 'once, one time', from /negə/ (stem /negən+/) 'one'; /gurbəntə/ 'thrice, three times' from /gurbəŋ/ (stem /gurbən+/) 'three'.

The same suffix is taken by /oləŋ/ 'many' and /xedəŋ/ 'several', e.g. /oləntə/ 'many times', from the stem /olən+/; /xedəntə/ 'several times', from the stem /xedən+/.

3.334. Adverbs from adverbs

Adverbs from adverbs are formed with the suffixes /+də/, /+gši/, and /+ɯɯr/, and the particle /č/ or /či/.

(1) /+də/, e.g. /xeʒeedə/ 'always', from /xeʒee/ 'when?'; /caašidə/ 'in the future', from /caaši/ 'further, in that direction'; /xoenəgšidə/ 'in the future', from /xoenəgši/ 'in the future'.

(2) /+gši/, e.g. /xoenəgši/ 'in the future', from /xoenə/ 'afterwards'; /gadəgši/ 'out', from /gadaa/ 'outside'.

(3) /+ɯɯr/, e.g. /gaduur/ 'along the outside, by', from /gadaa/ 'outside'; /caaguur/ 'farther off', from /caa/ in /caaši/ 'in that direction'.

(4) The indefinite adverbs are formed from the interrogative adverbs, see 3.252, by adding the particle /č/ or /či/, see 3.293, e.g. /xaač/ 'wherever', from /xaa/ 'where?'; /xeʒeeč/ 'whenever', from /xeʒee/ 'when?'.

3.335. Compound adverbs

There are four main types of compound adverbs: (1) reduplication of the adverb; (2) compounds composed of an adverb preceded by another adverb; (3) compounds composed of an adverb preceded by an emphasizing adverb; and (4) compounds of an adverb followed by an echoing word.

(1) Reduplication, e.g. /xaaxaa/ 'where where?'.

(2) Adverb preceded by another adverb which has the opposite meaning, e.g. /endətəndə/ 'here and there, somewhere', from /endə/ 'here' and /tendə/ 'there'.

(3) Adverb preceded by an emphasizing adverb, see 3.254, e.g. /xeb xeʒee/ 'whenever, always', from /xeb/ and /xeʒee/ 'when?'.

(4) Adverb followed by an echoing word, e.g. /araečirae/ 'somehow, scarcely', from /arae/ 'hardly, scarcely'.

3.34. Verbs

Verbs are formed from nouns, adjectives, numerals, adverbs, verbs, and interjections.

3.341. Verbs from nouns

(1) /+l-/ or /+lə-/ forms verbs from noun stems, except those ending in /m/ or /ŋ/ (see [2] below). The verbs derived with this suffix are mostly transitive and have the general meanings "to do or to employ something, to act as something", e.g. /gaʒərlə-/ 'to put into the earth, to bury', from /gaʒər/ 'earth'; /orlə-/ 'to replace someone, to be someone's deputy', from /or/ (stem /orən+/) 'place'; /altəl-/ 'to gild', from /altə/ (stem /altən+/) 'gold'; /dael-/ 'to wage war', from /daeŋ/ (stem /daen+/) 'war'; /gaʒərčil-/ 'to guide, to be a guide', from /gaʒərči/ 'guide'; /usəl-/ 'to water', from /us/ (stem /usən+/) 'water'; /šubuul-/ 'to hunt birds' from /šubuu/ (stem /šubuun+/) 'bird'.

(2) /+nə-/, with noun stems ending in /m/ or /ŋ/. The stem-final /ŋ/ of the noun is replaced by /g/, e.g. /emnə-/ 'to cure, to treat', from /em/ 'medicine'; /gamnə-/ 'to take good care of something, to use sparingly, to keep something', from /gam/ 'thrift, careful handling, care for something'; /agnə-/ 'to hunt', from /aŋ/ (stem /aŋ+/) 'game animal'.

(3) /+də-/ typically forms transitive verbs having the general meaning "to use or employ something", e.g. /gaʒərdə-/ 'to land', from /gazər/ 'land, earth'; /argədə-/ 'to use a ruse', from /argə/ 'ruse, means, trick'; /algədə-/ 'to slap', from /aləg/ (stem /aləgən+/) 'palm of the hand'.

(4) /+tə-/ typically forms intransitive verbs with the general meaning "to become something", e.g. /gemtə-/ 'to be damaged, to suffer damage', from /gem/ 'evil, damage'; /xirtə-/ 'to become dusty, filthy, or soiled', from /xir/ 'filth'; /tosətə-/ 'to become greasy, to be soiled with grease', from /tos/ (stem /tosən+/) 'grease, fat'.

(5) /+ǰi-/ forms intransitive verbs with the general meaning "to become something", e.g. /urəǰi-/ 'to procreate, to increase in number', from /urə/ 'fruit, seed, offspring'; /amərǰi-/ 'to calm down, to be in peace', from /amər/ 'peace'.

(6) /+ǰirə-/ forms intransitive verbs with the same meanings as (5), e.g. /aŋgiǰirə-/ 'to be separated from something, to get rid of something', from /aŋgi/ 'part, division, class'.

(7) /+rə-/ forms intransitive verbs with the same meanings as (5) and (6), e.g. /enčirə-/ 'to become orphaned', from /enčiŋ/ (stem /enčin+/) 'orphan'; /belbəsrə-/ 'to be widowed', from /belbəs/ (stem /belbəsən+/) 'widower, widow'.

(8) /+ši-/ forms intransitive verbs with the general meaning "to acquire something", e.g. /aldərši-/ 'to become famous, to acquire fame', from /aldər/ 'fame'; /suuriši-/ 'to become sedentary, to settle down and cease to be a nomad', from /suuri/ 'seat, place'.

(9) /+širə-/ forms intransitive verbs with the same meanings as (8), e.g. /ʒugširə-/ 'to get into the habit of something, to grow familiar with something', from /ʒug/ 'direction'; /sanaaširə-/ 'to intend', from /sanaa/ (stem /sanaan+/) 'thought'.

(10) /+rxə-/ forms intransitive verbs with the general meaning "to possess a certain quality in excess", e.g. /noyərxə-/ 'to be fond of power, to be imperious or tyrannical', from /noyəŋ/ (stem /noyən+/) 'prince'; /omərxə-/ 'to be haughty', from /oməg/ 'pride, haughtiness'.

(11) /+sǝ-/ forms intransitive verbs, e.g. /noersǝ-/ 'to
ɛleep', from /noer/ 'sleep'; /maxǝsǝ-/ 'to crave after meat',
from /maxǝ/ (stem /maxǝn+/) 'meat'.

3.342. Verbs from adjectives

Verbs from adjectives are formed with the suffixes enumerated
in 3.341, and a few other suffixes.

(1) /+s-/ forms intransitive verbs, e.g. /nariis-/ 'to
become thin', from /nariiŋ/ (stem /nariin+/) 'thin'; /bagǝs-/
'to become small', from /bagǝ/ 'small'.

(2) /+dǝ-/, cf. above, e.g. /yixǝdǝ-/ 'to become large,
to increase' from /yixǝ/ 'large, great'; /urtǝdǝ-/ 'to become
long', from /urtǝ/ 'long'.

(3) /+rǝ-/, cf. above, e.g. /xǝxǝrǝ-/ 'to become blue',
from /xǝxǝ/ 'blue'; /nogoorǝ-/ 'to become green' from /nogooŋ/
(stem /nogoon+/) 'green'.

(4) /+l-/, cf. above, with stems containing the phoneme
/r/, forms verbs with the same meanings as (3), e.g. /šarǝl-/
'to become yellow', from /šar/ ~ /šarǝ/ 'yellow'.

(5) /+ji-/ forms intransitive verbs, cf. above, e.g.
/bayǝji-/ 'to become rich', from /bayǝŋ/ (stem /bayǝn+/) 'rich';
/ǝnǝrji-/ 'to become a member of a large family, to become a
member of a large group of people mutually related', from /ǝnǝr/
'having a large family'; /mergǝji-/ 'to specialize, to acquire a
specialty', from /mergǝŋ/ (stem /mergǝn+/) 'wise'.

(6) /+jirǝ-/ forms intransitive verbs, cf. above, e.g.
/saejirǝ-/ 'to improve', from /saeŋ/ (stem /saen+/) 'good';
/muujirǝ-/ 'to deteriorate', from /muu/ 'bad'.

(7) /+šee-/ forms transitive verbs with the general meaning "to regard as something", e.g. /saešaa-/ 'to approve of',
from /saeŋ/ (stem /saen+/) 'good'; /ʒebšee-/ 'to approve of, to
regard as correct', from /ʒeb/ 'correct, just'; /buruušaa-/ 'to
reproach, to censure', from /buruu/ 'wrong'.

(8) /+čil-/ forms transitive verbs, e.g. /šinǝčil-/ 'to
renew', from /šinǝ/ 'new'.

(9) /+šírə-/ forms intransitive verbs, cf. above, e.g. /oləšírə-/ 'to increase, to grow numerous', from /oləŋ/ (stem /olən+/) 'many, numerous'; /taebəšírə-/ 'to calm down, to become peaceful', from /taebəŋ/ (stem /taebən+/) 'peaceful'.

3.343. Verbs from numerals

(1) /+də-/, cf. above, e.g. /xoyərdə-/ 'to bifurcate, to hesitate between two solutions', from /xoyər/ 'two'; /gurbədə-/ 'to make threefold', from /gurbəŋ/ (stem /gurbən+/) 'three'.

(2) /+tə-/, cf. above, e.g. /xoyərtə-/ 'to be split into two, to see double', from /xoyər/ 'two'.

3.344. Verbs from adverbs

Verbs from adverbs are formed with the suffixes /+1-/, /+rə-/, /+čí-/, and /+čil-/.

(1) /+1-/, cf. above, e.g. /gadaal-/ 'to go outside', from /gadaa/ 'out'; /caašil-/ 'to proceed further, to move in that direction', from /caaší/ 'farther away, in that direction'; /multəl-/ 'to pull out', from /multə/ 'out, off'; /butəl-/ 'to break to small pieces, to crush', from /butə/ 'asunder'.

(2) /+rə-/, cf. above, e.g. /multər-/ 'to fall out', from /multə/ 'out, off'; /ʒadərə-/ 'to split open', from /ʒadə/ 'openly, gapingly'.

(3) /+čí-/ forms transitive verbs, e.g. /ʒugəčí-/ 'to pull out, to jerk out', from /sugə/ 'out'; /multəčí-/ 'to pull out with a sudden and sharp movement', from /multə/ 'out, off'.

(4) /+čil-/, cf. above, forms transitive verbs, e.g. /gaduurčil-/ 'to regard someone as a stranger, to have the feeling that someone does not belong where he is, to discriminate', from /gaduur/ 'out, along the outer side'.

3.345. Verbs from verbs

Verbs from verbs can be divided into two main groups: (1) verbs which can be formed from all verbal stems, and (2) verbs which can only be formed from a limited number of verbal stems.

3.3451. Verbs of the first category are comparable to the voices of the Latin, Greek, or English verb, e.g. active, passive (and in Greek, also middle) voice. In Mongolian this category comprises the causative, passive, cooperative, reciprocal, intensive, diminutive, and plural verbs.

3.34511. Causative (or factitive) verbs convey the idea of making someone perform an action. The suffixes are /-uɯl-/, /-guɯl-/, /-lgə-/, /-gə-/, /-xə-/, /-gee-/, and /-ee-/.

(1) /-uɯl-/ forms causative verbs from transitive verbs, and transitive verbs from intransitive verbs. It is added to stems ending in /ə/ and /i/, e.g. /yabuul-/ 'to make (let) go, to send', from /yabə-/ 'to go, to walk'; /uʒuɯl-/ 'to make see, to show', from /uʒə-/ 'to see'; /bičuɯl-/ 'to make write down', from /biči-/ 'to write'; /bariuul-/ 'to make seize, to hand', from /bari-/ 'to seize'; /iduɯl-/ 'to make (let) eat, to feed', from /idə-/ 'to eat'; /aluul-/ 'to make (let) kill', from /alə-/ 'to kill'; /oruul-/ 'to make (let) enter, to bring in', from /orə-/ ~ /or-/ 'to enter'.

(2) /-guɯl-/ is found in /baeguul-/ 'to establish, to found', from /bae-/ 'to be'.

(3) /-lgə-/ forms causative verbs from transitive verbs, and transitive verbs from intransitive verbs. It is added to stems ending in a geminate vowel phoneme or a diphthong, e.g. /uulgə-/ 'to make drink', from /uu-/ 'to drink'; /suulgə-/ 'to make (let) sit, to seat', from /suu-/ 'to sit'; /nuɯlgə-/ 'to make (let) move to another place, to cause someone to change his abode', from /nuɯ-/ 'to transhume, to live a nomad's life'; /xaraelgə-/ 'to make jump', from /xarae-/ 'to jump'; /baelgə-/ 'to let be somewhere, to leave somebody, to station', from /bae-/ 'to be'.

(4) /-gə-/ forms causative verbs from stems ending in /l r s/, e.g. /bolgə-/ 'to make', from /bol-/ 'to become'; /olgə-/ 'to make find, to hand out, to give', from /ol-/ 'to find'; /gargə-/ 'to make come out, to let out, to take out, to

chase out', from /gar-/ 'to come out'; /xɯrgə-/ 'to bring to
the point of destination', from /xɯr-/ 'to arrive, to reach';
/surgə-/ 'to teach, to instruct', from /sur-/ 'to learn,
to study'; /bosgə-/ 'to make stand up, to erect', from /bos-/
'to go up'.

(5) /-xə-/, which occurs in most dialects, is added to
stems ending in /s d/, e.g. /bosxə-/ 'to make stand up', from
/bos-/ 'to stand up', see above; /əsxə-/ 'to increase the number
of something, to breed, to raise cattle', from /əs-/ 'to increase
in number, to procreate'; /negədxə-/ 'to unite somebody', from
/negəd-/ ~ /negədə-/ 'to become one, to join'; /cadxə-/ 'to
satiate somebody', from /cad-/ 'to become satiated'.

(6) /-gee-/ is found on a few stems ending in /ə/, e.g.
/unəgaa-/ 'to make fall down, to overthrow', from /unə-/ 'to
fall down'.

(7) /-ee-/ is added to some stems ending in /ə/, e.g.
/ʒoboo-/ 'to torment', from /ʒobə-/ 'to suffer'; /untəraa-/ 'to
extinguish, to put out' (fire), from /untərə-/ 'to go out'
(light); /ʒogsoo-/ 'to stop', from /ʒogsə-/ 'to stand still';
/xataa-/ 'to make dry, to dry something', from /xatə-/ 'to become dry'.

3.34512. Passive verbs are formed with the suffixes /-gdə-/, and
/-də-/ or /-tə-/.

(1) /-gdə-/ is added to stems ending in /ə/, /i/, or a
geminate vowel phoneme, e.g. /barigdə-/ 'to be seized, to be
caught', from /bari-/ 'to seize, to catch'; /uʒəgdə-/ 'to be
seen', from /uʒə-/ 'to see'; /geegdə-/ 'to be lost, to get
lost'. from /gee-/ 'to lose'; /oroogdə-/ 'to be wrapped', from
/oroo-/ 'to wrap'; /aləgdə-/ 'to be killed', from /alə-/ 'to
kill'.

(2) /-də-/ is added to stems ending in /l/, /-tə-/ to
stems ending in /r b g/, e.g. /oldə-/ 'to be found', from /ol-/
'to find'; /gartə-/ 'to be excelled by someone, to be defeated
in horse races', from /gar-/ 'to excel, to win a race';

/abtə-/ 'to be taken', from /ab-/ 'to take'; /əgtə-/ 'to be given', from /əg-/ 'to give'.

3.34513. Cooperative verbs convey the idea of participation in an action or joining others in an action. The suffix is /-lcə-/, e.g. /idəlcə-/ 'to eat with others', from /idə-/ 'to eat'; /suulcə-/ 'to sit with others, to attend a session', from /suu-/ 'to sit'; /surəlcə-/ 'to study in a group with others', from /sur-/ 'to study'.

3.34514. Reciprocal verbs convey the idea of an action directed against each other by the actors. The suffix is /-ldə-/, e.g. /buudəldə-/ 'to shoot at each other', from /buudə-/ 'to shoot'; /aləldə-/ 'to kill each other', from /alə-/ 'to kill'; /barildə-/ 'to seize each other, to wrestle', from /bari-/ 'to seize'; /tebrəldə-/ 'to embrace each other', from /tebrə-/ 'to embrace'.

3.34515. Intensive verbs denote actions which affect the object totally, or actions carried out completely and to the very end. The suffixes are /-či-/ and /-čxə-/.

  (1) /-či-/ is added to intransitive verbs, e.g. /yabəči-/ 'to leave, go away', from /yabə-/ 'to go'; /untəči-/ 'to fall asleep', from /untə-/ 'to sleep'.

  (2) /-čxə-/ is added to transitive verbs, e.g. /idəčxə-/ 'to eat up', from /idə-/ 'to eat'; /buudəčxə-/ 'to shoot to death', from /buudə-/ 'to shoot'.

3.34516. Diminutive verbs denote actions of short duration. The suffix is /-ʒənə-/, e.g. /suuʒənə-/ 'to sit down for a while', from /suu-/ 'to sit'; /xɯleeʒənə-/ 'to wait a little', from /xɯlee-/ 'to wait'; /baeʒənə-/ 'to stop for a while, to wait', from /bae-/ 'to be, to stand'.

3.34517. Plural verbs denote actions performed by many actors. The suffix is /-cəgee-/, e.g. /yabəcəgaa-/ 'to walk, to go',

111

from /yabə-/ 'to walk, to go'; /suucəgaa-/ 'to sit, to live' (many persons), from /suu-/ 'to sit, to live' (one person); /orəcəgoo-/ 'to enter' (many persons), from /orə-/ 'to enter'.

3.34518. The suffixes enumerated in sections 3.34511-3.34517 may combine with one another. Thus, a causative verb may be formed from a reciprocal verb; a passive verb may be formed from a causative verb, etc. However, there are restrictions on which suffixes may be added to each other.

(1) A causative verb may be formed from a primary verb stem, a causative verb, a passive verb, a cooperative verb, or a reciprocal verb.

(a) Causative from a primary stem, e.g. /iruɯl-/ 'to make come', from /irə-/ 'to come'.

(b) Causative from a causative, e.g. /oruulgə-/ 'to make bring in', from /oruul-/ 'to make come in, to bring in', from /orə-/ 'to go in'; /garguul-/ 'to make take out', from /gargə-/ 'to take out', from /gar-/ 'to go out'.

(c) Causative from a passive, e.g. /ɯrəgduɯl-/ 'to waste, to squander', from /ɯrəgdə-/ 'to be spent', from /ɯrə-/ 'to spend'; /barigduul-/ 'to cause to be seized', from /barigdə-/ 'to be seized', from /bari-/ 'to seize'; /barəgduul-/ 'to cause to decrease', from /barəgdə-/ 'to be exhausted, to be spent', from /barə-/ 'to end, to come to an end'.

(d) Causative from a cooperative, e.g. /orəlcuul-/ 'to make participate', from /orəlcə-/ 'to participate, to enter with the others', from /orə-/ 'to enter'.

(e) Causative from a reciprocal, e.g. /barilduul-/ 'to make wrestle', from /barildə-/ 'to wrestle', from /bari-/ 'to seize'.

(2) A passive verb can only be formed from a primary or a causative verb.

(a) Passive from a primary stem, e.g. /aləgdə-/ 'to be killed', from /alə-/ 'to kill'.

(b) Passive from a causative, e.g. /togtoogdʉ-/ 'to be resolved', from /togtoo-/ 'to resolve', from /togtə-/ 'to stand'; /baeguuləgdə-/ 'to be founded', from /baeguul-/ 'to found', from /bae-/ 'to be'.

(3) A cooperative verb can be formed from a primary verb, a causative verb, or a reciprocal verb.

(a) Cooperative from a primary stem, e.g. /suulcə-/ 'to participate in something, to sit together with other persons, to attend a meeting', from /suu-/ 'to sit down'.

(b) Cooperative from a causative, e.g. /baeguuləlcə-/ 'to participate in founding or erecting something', from /baeguul-/ 'to found', from /bae-/ 'to be'.

(c) Cooperative from a reciprocal, e.g. /buudəldəlcə-/ 'to participate in shooting at each other', from /buudəldə-/ 'to shoot at each other', from /buudə-/ 'to shoot'.

(4) A reciprocal verb can be formed only from a primary verb, e.g. /aləldə-/ 'to kill each other', from /alə-/ 'to kill'.

(5) Intensive verbs can be formed from most verbs, e.g. /aləčxə-/, from /alə-/ 'to kill'; /gargəčxə-/, from /gargə-/ 'to take out', from /gar-/ 'to go out'; /gartəči-/, from /gartə-/ 'to be excelled', from /gar-/ 'to excel'.

(6) Plural verbs can be formed from all verbs, e.g. /suucəgaa-/, from /suu-/ 'to sit'; /ʊʒʊʊlcəgee-/, from /ʊʒʊʊl-/ 'to show', from /ʊʒə-/ 'to see'; /aləgdəcəgaa-/, from /aləgdə-/ 'to be killed', from /alə-/ 'to kill'; /idəlcəcəgee-/, from /idəlcə-/ 'to participate in eating', from /idə-/ 'to eat'; /barildəcəgaa-/, from /barildə-/ 'to wrestle', from /bari-/ 'to seize'.

3.3452. Verbs of the second category cannot be formed from all verbs.

(1) /-l-/ forms frequentative verbs, i.e. verbs denoting
actions which are repeated without interruption, e.g. /dusəl-/
'to drip', from /dusə-/ 'to drop, to fall' (drops); /coxil-/
'to knock all the time', from /coxi-/ 'to strike, to beat'.

(2) /-rə-/ forms middle verbs, i.e. verbs which denote
actions which take place without being caused by an actor, i.e.
actions which, so to speak, take place all by themselves, e.g.
/ebdərə-/ 'to fall to pieces, to get broken', from /ebdə-/ 'to
break'; /asxərə-/ 'to spill' (intr.), from /asxə-/ 'to spill
something'.

(3) /-lẑə-/ forms verbs which denote rhythmic motions,
e.g. /gaŋxəlẑə-/ 'to swing' (branches of a tree), from /gaŋxə-/
'to swing'.

(4) /-bəlẑə-/ or /-gəlẑə-/ forms verbs which denote un-
interrupted actions, e.g. /anibəlẑə-/ 'to blink all the time',
from /ani-/ 'to close the eyes'; /sanəgəlẑə-/ 'to daydream',
from /sanə-/ 'to think'.

3.346. Verbs from interjections

Verbs from interjections are formed with the suffixes /+čignə-/,
/+ginə-/ or /+gəna-/, and /+xirə-/ or /+xərə-/. They denote the
making of sounds for which the interjection in question stands.

(1) /+čignə-/, e.g. /tarčignə-/ 'to jingle, to crackle',
from /tar/; /šarčignə-/ 'to rustle', from /šar/.

(2) /+ginə-/ or /+gənə-/, e.g. /xaŋginə-/ 'to ring, to
clank', from /xaŋ/; /giŋginə-/ 'to make a thin and wailing sound',
from /giŋ/; /dɯŋginə-/ 'to drone', from /dɯŋ/.

(3) /+xirə-/ or /+xərə-/, e.g. /xašxərə-/ 'to shout', from
/xaš/; /barxirə-/ 'to shout, yell, cry', from /bar/; /xurxirə-/
'to snore, to snort', from /xur/.

3.347. Compound verbs

Compound verbs are composed of an adverb or interjection and the
verb /xii-/ 'to do'.

(1) Adverbs in /-s/ (formed from verb stems) and /xii-/
yield verbs denoting quick and often unexpected actions, e.g.
/cuxəsxii-/ 'to pop up quickly and unexpectedly', from /cuxui-/
'to appear, to protrude'; /yabəsxii-/ 'to go quickly', from
/yabə-/ 'to go'.

(2) Interjections and /xii-/, e.g. /xoŋxii-/ 'to ring',
from /xoŋ/; /šarxii-/ 'to rustle', from /šar/.

3.4. Inflection

3.41. Noun inflection

Nouns may occur unsuffixed or with one or more inflectional suffixes. There are three kinds of suffixes which may be added to
noun stems, namely, plural suffixes, declensional suffixes, and
possessive suffixes, in this order. In addition, short forms
of the personal pronouns may be added enclitically. They function as possessive suffixes.

3.411. Basic form

A noun without any suffixes is the basic form. It is identical
with the stem. Nouns ending in /n/ which alternates with zero
have two stems: the plural suffixes and some declension suffixes are added to the stem which lacks the final /n/; the
other declension suffixes are added to the stem ending in /n/.

3.412. Plural suffixes

There are several plural suffixes.

(1) /+d/ is added to noun stems which end in /n/ and in
/n/ ~ zero, and to stems formed with the suffixes /+či/, /-eeči/,
and /-gči/.

> /noyəd/ 'princes', from /noyən+/
> /morid/ 'horses', from /morin+/ ~ /mori+/
> /malčid/ 'cattlemen', from /malčin+/
> /galčid/ 'firemen', from /galči+/

115

/bičeečid/ 'scribes', from /bičeeči+/

/surəgčid/ 'students', from /surəgči+/

The plural of /nøxər+/ 'comrade, friend' is /nøxəd/; the plural of /tuّsiməl+/ 'official' is /tuّsiməd/.

(2) /+s/ is added to noun stems which end in /ə/, in a geminate vowel phoneme, and to some stems which end in the diphthongs /ae/ and /oe/. The diphthongs are shortened to /ə/.

/dargəs/ 'chiefs', from /dargə+/

/erəs/ 'men', from /erə+/

/ʒaluus/ 'young men', from /ʒaluu+/

/gaxəs/ 'hogs', from /gaxae+/

/noxəs/ 'dogs', from /noxoe+/

(3) /+nuɯd/ is added to most noun stems which end in the diphthongs /ae/ and /oe/, and in the geminate vowel phonemes /ee/ and /ii/.

/dalaenuud/ 'seas', from /dalae+/

/xooloenuud/ 'pipes', from /xooloe+/

/degeenuɯd/ 'hooks', from /degee+/

/erbeexiinuɯd/ 'butterflies', from /erbeexii+/

(4) /+uɯd/ is added to noun stems which end in consonants other than /n/.

/xøləguɯd/ 'vessels', from /xələg+/

/arəduud/ 'cattlemen, free nomads', from /arəd+/

/tələbuɯd/ 'forms', from /tələb+/

/ulsuud/ 'peoples, nations', from /uləs+/

/aŋguud/ 'game animals', from /aŋ+/

(5) /+nər/ is added to stems of nouns which denote various degrees of kinship, senior and respected persons, and gods. The suffix is rendered as **нар** in orthography and written separately.

/axənər/ 'elder brothers', from /axə+/

/duɯunər/ 'younger brothers', from /duɯu+/

/beenər/ 'shamans', from /bee+/

/la/mənər/ 'Buddhist priests', from /lamə+/

/bagšinər/ 'teachers', from /bagši+/

/teŋrinər/ 'gods', from /teŋri+/

/bodisəduaanər/ 'the Bodhisattvas', from /bodisəduaa+/

(6) To plural forms ending in /+s/, /+d/, and /+nər/ the suffix /+ɯɯd/ may be added. Such double plural forms are used with reference to esteemed persons, e.g. /ersɯɯd/ 'men', from /erəs/, from /erə+/; /noyəduud/ 'princes', from /noyəd/, from /noyən+/; /nexədɯɯd/ 'comrades', from /nexəd/, from /nexər+/; /lamənəruud/ 'Buddhist priests', from /lamənər/, from /lamə+/.

3.413. Declension suffixes

Mongolian has eight cases, namely, subject-direct object, genitive, dative-locative, ablative, accusative, instrumental, comitative, and directive.

The case suffixes are added to the stem. With stems ending in /n/ alternating with zero, the genitive, dative-locative, and ablative suffixes are added to the stem with final /n/. The other case suffixes are added to the stem lacking the final /n/.

The case suffixes are the same for both the singular and plural. In the singular, they are added directly to the stem. In the plural, they are added after the plural suffix.

(1) The subject-direct object case is formed with a zero suffix, i.e. it is identical with the stem. Nouns ending in /n/ ~ zero use the stem without /n/.

/mori/ 'horse', from /morin+/ ~ /mori+/

/noyəŋ/ 'prince', from /noyən+/

/ger/ 'yurt', from /ger+/

/nom/ 'book', from /nom+/

(2) The genitive case is formed with the suffixes /+n/, /+iin/, /+giin/, /+ii/. The final /n/ of /+n +iin +giin/ becomes /ŋ/ in word-final position, but remains /n/ before /+də/; see 3.4131.

(a) /+ŋ/ is added to stems ending in /ii/ or diphthongs.

/delxiiŋ/ 'of the world', from /delxii+/

/dalaeŋ/ 'of the sea', from /dalae+/

/noxoeŋ/ 'of the dog', from /noxoe+/

/xarəŋxuiŋ/ 'of the darkness', from /xarəŋxui+/

(b) /+iiŋ/ is added to front-vocalic stems ending in /ə/ or in any consonant except /n/; to back-vocalic stems ending in /g/; and to stems with back or front vowels which end in /i/. The allomorph /+əiiŋ/ is added to back-vocalic stems ending in /ə/, or in /b d s m l r/.

/eriiŋ/ 'of the man', from /erə+/

/teləbiiŋ/ 'of the form', from /teləb+/

/ediiŋ/ 'of material', from /ed+/

/besiiŋ/ 'of the textile', from /bes+/

/emiiŋ/ 'of the medicine', from /em+/

/emeeliiŋ/ 'of the saddle', from /emeel+/

/geriiŋ/ 'of the yurt', from /ger+/

/bičigiiŋ/ 'of the writing', from /bičig+/

/adəgiiŋ/ 'of the lower course of the river', from /adəg+/

/aŋgiiŋ/ 'of the game animal', from /aŋ+/ ~ /aŋg+/

/bičeečiiŋ/ 'of the scribe', from /bičeeči/

/surguuliiŋ/ 'of the school', from /surguuli+/

/bagšiiŋ/ 'of the teacher', from /bagši+/

/mujiiŋ/ 'of the province', from /muji+/

/axəiiŋ/ 'of the elder brother', from /axə+/

/xadəiiŋ/ 'of the cliff', from /xadə+/

/xabəiiŋ/ 'of the Pekingese' (dog), from /xab+/

/moridəiiŋ/ 'of the horses', from /morid+/, from /morin+/ ~ /mori+/

/uləsəiiŋ/ 'of the nation', from /uləs+/

/saməiiŋ/ 'of the comb', from /sam+/

/galəiiŋ/ 'of the fire', from /gal+/

/garəiiŋ/ 'of the hand', from /gar+/

(c) /+giiŋ/ is added to stems ending in a front or back geminate vowel phoneme.

118

/bɵɵgiiŋ/ 'of the shaman', from /bɵɵ+/

/eleegiiŋ/ 'of the vulture', from /elee+/

/odoogiiŋ/ 'of the present time', from /odoo+/

(d) /+ii/ is added to stems with front vowels which end
in /n/. The allomorph /+əii/ is added to stems with
back vowels which end in /n/.

/xelnii/ 'of the tongue', from /xelən+/ ~ /xelə+/

/ɯsənii/ 'of the hair', from /ɯsən+/ ~ /ɯsə+/

/modənəii/ 'of the tree', from /modən+/ ~ /modə+/

/noyənəii/ 'of the prince', from /noyən+/

(3) The dative-locative case is formed with the suffix
/+də/, added to stems which end in a vowel or diphthong or in
/ŋ n m l/. Stems ending in any other consonant take the allomorph /+tə/.

/axədə/ 'to the elder brother', from /axə+/

/aŋdə/ 'to the game animal', from /aŋ+/ ~ /aŋg+/

/noyəndə/ 'to the prince', from /noyən+/

/morində/ 'to the horse', from /morin+/ ~ /mori+/

/emdə/ 'to the medicine', from /em+/

/bičigtə/ 'to the writing', from /bičig+/

/uləstə/ 'to the nation', from /uləs+/

/gertə/ 'in the yurt', from /ger+/

(4) The ablative case is formed with the suffix /-ees/,
added to all stems with the exception of those ending in a
geminate vowel phoneme or a diphthong, which take the allomorph
/+gees/.

/axaas/ 'from the elder brother', from /axə+/

/garaas/ 'from the hand', from /gar+/

/tɯšiməlees/ 'from the official', from /tɯšiməl+/

/aŋgaas/ 'from the game animal', from /aŋ+/ ~ /aŋg+/

/dɯɯgees/ 'from the younger brother', from /dɯɯ+/

/morinoos/ 'from the horse', from /morin+/ ~ /mori+/

/dalaegaas/ 'from the sea', from /dalae+/

(5) The accusative, the case of the definite direct object
(see 4.152), is formed with the suffixes /+g/ and /+iig/.

119

(a) /+g/ is added to stems ending in a geminate vowel phoneme or a diphthong; also to stems ending in /n/ ∼ zero preceded by a geminate vowel phoneme.

/bөөg/ 'the shaman', from /bөө+/

/toog/ 'the number', from /toon+/ ∼ /too+/

/galuug/ 'the goose', from /galuun+/ ∼ /galuu+/

/dalaeg/ 'the sea', from /dalae+/

(b) /+iig/ is added to stems with front vowels which end in any consonant or in /ə/ or /i/, and to stems with back vowels which end in /i/ or /g/. Back-vocalic stems ending in /ə/ or any consonant other than /g/ take the allomorph /+əiig/.

/bičigiig/ 'the letter', from /bičig+/

/eriig/ 'the man', from /erə+/

/emiig/ 'the medicine', from /em+/

/emeeliig/ 'the saddle', from /emeel+/

/surguuliig/ 'the school', from /surguuli+/

/adəgiig/ 'the lower course of the river', from /adəg+/

/aŋgiig/ 'the game animal', from /aŋ+/ ∼ /aŋg+/

/garəiig/ 'the hand', from /gar+/

/axəiig/ 'the elder brother', from /axə+/

(6) The instrumental case is formed with the suffix /+eer/. Stems ending in a geminate vowel phoneme or a diphthong take the allomorph /+geer/.

/nexərөөr/ 'with the help of the comrade', from /nexər+/

/sɯxeer/ 'by means of an ax', from /sɯxə+/

/garaar/ 'by means of the hand', from /gar+/

/aŋgaar/ 'by means of a game animal', from /aŋ+/ ∼ /aŋg+/

/morioor/ 'by horse', from /morin+/ ∼ /mori+/

/dɯɯgeer/ 'with the help of the younger brother', from
    /dɯɯ+/

/dalaegaar/ 'by sea', from /dalae+/

(7) The comitative case is formed with the suffix /+tee ∼ +tae ∼ +toe/.

/aabətae/ 'with the father', from /aabə+/

/nəxərtee/ 'with the comrade', from /nəxər+/

/noxoetoe/ 'with the dog', from /noxoe+/

(8) The directive case is formed with the suffix /+rɯɯ/.
With stems containing /r/ the suffix is /+lɯɯ/.

/usəruu/ 'towards the water', from /usən+/ ~ /usə+/

/dargəluu/ 'in the direction of the chief', from /dargə+/

/gerlɯɯ/ 'in the direction of the house', from /ger+/

/cecəgrɯɯ/ 'in the direction of the flowers', from /cecəg+/

3.4131. Certain case suffixes may be added to other case suffixes.
The resulting forms are called "double case forms". Such double
case forms are the genitive-locative, locative-ablative, and
the genitive-directive. Almost any case suffix may be added to
a comitative form.

(1) The genitive-locative is formed with a genitive suffix to which the suffix of the dative-locative is added. Consequently, the compound suffixes are /+ndə/, /+iində/, /+əiində/,
/+giində/, /+iidə/, /+əiidə/ (the last is usually /+aedə/,
/+oedə/).

/badəmguaendə/ 'at Mr. Badma's', from /badəmguaeŋ/

/bagšiində/ 'at the teacher's', from /bagši+/

/laməiində/ 'at the lama's', from /lamə+/

/noyənoedə/ 'at the prince's', from /noyən+/

(2) The locative-ablative is formed with the suffixes
/+də/ and /+ees/. Only the word /ger/ 'house' occurs in this
form, which is /gertees/ 'from home'.

(3) The genitive-directive is identical in meaning with
the directive. It is formed with the directive suffix, which
is added to the genitive suffix, e.g. /axəiinruu/ 'in the direction of the elder brother'.

(4) The comitative form takes all case suffixes. The most
frequent compound forms are the comitative-accusative, e.g.
/axətaeg/ 'with the elder brother', and the comitative-

instrumental (identical in meaning with the simple comitative),
e.g. /axətaegaar/ 'together with the elder brother'.

3.414. Possessive suffixes

The possessive suffixes indicate the owner or possessor of the
object concerned. They are added to the case suffixes. There
are two kinds of possessive suffixes, namely, a personal possessive suffix, and a reflexive possessive suffix.

Abbreviated forms of the genitive case of the personal
pronouns may be added enclitically to the case forms to indicate possession. Although the short forms are not suffixes,
they will be dealt with in the following sections.

3.4141. The possessive suffix of the third person is /+ni/ after
vowels, /+ini/ after a final /n/, and /+əni/ after a consonant
other than /n/. The final /i/ of the suffix is usually dropped,
so that the suffix is /+n/, /+in/, or /+ən/, respectively. It
is to be noted that the final /n/ of the suffix is apico-dental,
not velar.

/axən/ 'his elder brother', from /axə+/
/noyənin/ 'his prince', from /noyən+/
/gerən/ 'his yurt', from /ger+/

The suffix /+n/, /+in/, /+ən/ is written as **нь** in the
Cyrillic script and always separately, e.g. **ах нь** /axən/ 'his
elder brother'.

3.4142. Possession by the first or second person is indicated by
the short genitive forms of the personal pronouns added enclitically to the case forms.

1st pers. sing. /mini/	1st pers. pl. /mani/ or /maani/
2nd pers. sing. /čini/	2nd pers. pl. /tani/ or /taani/

The final /i/ of all these forms is usually dropped, and
the form concerned ends in an apico-dental /n/, i.e. /min/ 'my',
/čin/ 'thy', /man/ or /maan/ 'our', /tan/ or /taan/ 'your'.

According to the rules of Mongolian orthography, the short genitive forms of pronouns are written separately, e.g. **ах минь** /axəmin/ 'my elder brother', with compound juncture between the stem and the short genitive form of the pronoun.

3.4143. The possessive suffix /+n/, etc. and the short genitive forms /min/, etc. are added to the case suffixes. Some case suffixes undergo changes.

    (1) The genitive suffixes ending in /n/ drop the /n/ before the suffix /+n/ and before /min/ and /man/, e.g.:

> gen. /+n/ + /+n/ → /+n/
>   + /min/ → /+min/
>   + /maan/ → /+maan/

In the orthography, the final /n/ of the genitive suffix is always written.

    (2) The accusative suffix /+iig/ ~ /+əiig/ drops its final /g/ before the suffix /+n/ and all enclitically added pronouns; the accusative suffix /+g/ is replaced with /+gii/, e.g.:

> acc. /+iig/ + /min/ → /+iimin/
>   + /čin/ → /+iičin/
>   + /+n/ → /+iin/
> acc. /+g/ + /min/ → /+giimin/
>   + /čin/ → /+giičin/
>   + /+n/ → /+giin/

    (3) The remaining case suffixes do not undergo any changes, e.g. abl. /+ees/ and /+ən/ result in /+eesən/ "from his..."; instr. /+eer/ and /min/ result in /+eermin/ "by means of my..."; dat.-loc. /+də/ and /čin/ result in /+dəčin/ "to thy..." or "in thy..."; comit. /+tae/ and /taan/ result in /+taetaan/ "together with your..."

3.4144. The reflexive possessive suffix, /+ee/ ~ /+gee/ ~ /+xee/ 'his, your, my...', indicates that the possessor of the object is the same as the subject of the sentence. The reflexive

possessive suffix may be added to any of the case suffixes but
the nominative, except for the reflexive nouns /ᴇᴇr+/ 'self'
and /ᴇᴇrsəd+/ 'selves' (see 3.212), which can function as the
subject of a sentence.

(1) /+ee/ is added to the accusative, dative-locative,
ablative, and instrumental suffixes; it may also be added directly to the noun stem to form an accusative. Final /n/ alternating with zero is dropped before the suffix.

(2) /+gee/ is added to the comitative and directive suffixes.

(3) /+xee/ is added to the genitive suffix.

3.41441. The reflexive possessive declension rules are illustrated
by the following examples.

nom.	/noxoe+/ 'dog'	/morin+/ ~ /mori+/ 'horse'	/ger+/ 'yurt'
gen.	/noxoeŋxoo/	/morinəiixoo/	/geriiŋxee/
acc.	/noxoegoo/	/moriigoo/ or	/geriigee/ or
		/morioo/	/geree/
dat.	/noxoedoo/	/morindoo/	/gertee/
abl.	/noxoegoosoo/	/morinoosoo/	/gereesee/
instr.	/noxoegooroo/	/moriooroo/	/gereeree/
comit.	/noxoetoegoo/	/moritoegoo/	/gerteegee/
dir.	/noxoeruugaa/	/moriluugaa/	/gerluɯgee/

3.42. Pronoun inflection

The inflection of the pronouns is, in general, similar to that
of the nouns: some pronouns take plural suffixes, and all pronouns take declension suffixes and possessive suffixes. The
main difference between the inflection of pronouns and that of
nouns is that each pronoun has more than one stem. Also, the
subject form is different from the declension stems and, therefore, the term nominative case is appropriate. In addition,
short genitive forms of the pronouns of the first or second
person may be used to indicate possession; see 3.414.

3.421. Personal pronouns

(1) The pronoun /bi/ 'I' has the declension stems /min+/, /namae+/, and /nadə+/.

nom.	/bi/ 'I'
gen.	/minii/
acc.	/namaeg/
dat.	/nadədə/
abl.	/nadaas/
instr.	/nadaar/
comit.	/nadətae/
dir.	/nadəruu/

(2) The pronoun /či/ 'thou' has the declension stems /čin+/, /čamae+/, and /čamə+/.

nom.	/či/ 'thou'
gen.	/činii/
acc.	/čamaeg/
dat.	/čamədə/
abl.	/čamaas/
instr.	/čamaar/
comit.	/čamətae/
dir.	/čaməruu/

(3) The pronoun /bidə/ 'we' has the declension stems /bidən+/ ~ /bidənər+/ and /man+/. The stem /bidən+/ ~ /bidənər+/ is an inclusive pronoun, i.e. "we the speakers and you the listeners"; the stem /man+/ is an exclusive pronoun, i.e. "we the speakers, excluding you the listeners". (Note that /bidənər+/ is a pleonastic plural, i.e. /bidə/ plus the plural suffix /+nər/.)

nom.	/bidə/	~ /bidənər/ 'we (incl.)'	/bidə/ 'we (excl.)'
gen.	/bidə̃nii/	~ /bidənəriiŋ/	/manae/
acc.	/bidəniig/	~ /bidənəriig/	/manəiig/
dat.	/bidəndə/	~ /bidənərtə/	/mandə/
abl.	/bidənees/	~ /bidənərees/	/manaas/
instr.	/bidəneer/	~ /bidənəreer/	/manaar/

comit. /bidəntee/ ~ /bidənərtee/   /mantae/

dir.   /bidənrɯɯ/ ~ /bidənərlɯɯ/   /manaeruu/

    (4) The pronoun /ta/ 'you (sing.)' has the declension stem /tan+/. Its plural is /taanər/, i.e. /taa+/ plus the plural suffix /+nər/.

nom.	/ta/ 'you (sing.)'	/taanər/ 'you (plur.)'
gen.	/tanae/	/taanərəiiŋ/
acc.	/tanəiig/	/taanərəiig/
dat.	/tạndə/	/taanərtə/
abl.	/tanaas/	/taanəraas/
instr.	/tanaar/	/taanəraar/
comit.	/tantae/	/taanərtae/
dir.	/tanaeruu/	/taanərluu/

    This pronoun also has the plural forms /taanuud/ and /taanuus/. These are regarded as impolite forms of address.

3.422. Demonstrative pronouns

The demonstrative pronouns /enə/ 'this' and /terə/ 'that' are also used as personal pronouns of the third person.

    (1) The declension stems of /enə/ 'this, he, she, it' are /ɯɯn+/, /enɯɯn+/, and /enən+/, which are freely interchangeable.

nom.	/enə/		
gen.	/ɯɯnii/	/enɯɯnii/	/enənii/
acc.	/ɯɯniig/	/enɯɯniig/	/enəniig/
dat.	/ɯɯndə/	/enɯɯndə/	/enəndə/
abl.	/ɯɯnees/	/enɯɯnees/	/enənees/
instr.	/ɯɯneer/	/enɯɯneer/	--
	/ɯɯgeer/	/enɯɯgeer/	--
comit.	/ɯɯntee/	/enɯɯntee/	--
dir.	--	--	/enərɯɯ/

    The plural is /edə/ (declension stem /edən+/) 'these, they', which may take the plural suffixes /+nər/ or /+geer/.

nom.	/edə/	/edənər/	/edəgeer/
gen.	/edənii/	/edənəriiŋ/	/edəgeeriiŋ/

acc.	/edəniig/	/edənəriig/	/edəgeeriig/
dat.	/edəndə/	/edənərtə/	/edəgeertə/
abl.	/edənees/	/edənərees/	/edəgeerees/
instr.	/edəneer/	/edənəreer/	/edəgeereer/
comit.	/edəntee/	/edənərtee/	/edəgeertee/
dir.	/edərɯɯ/	/edənərlɯɯ/	/edəgeerlɯɯ/

(2) The declension stems of /terə/ 'that, he, she, it' are /tɯɯn+/, /terɯɯn+/, and /terən+/ or /tern+/. They are freely interchangeable.

nom.	/terə/		
gen.	/tɯɯnii/	/terɯɯnii/	/ternii/
acc.	/tɯɯniig/	/terɯɯniig/	/terniig/
dat.	/tɯɯndə/	/terɯɯndə/	--
abl.	/tɯɯnees/	/terɯɯnees/	/ternees/
instr. {	/tɯɯneer/	/terɯɯneer/	--
	/tɯɯgeer/	/terɯɯgeer/	--
comit.	/tɯɯntee/	/terɯɯntee/	--
dir.	--	--	/terəlɯɯ/

The plural is /tedə/ (declension stem /tedən+/) 'those, they', which may take the plural suffixes /+nər/ or /+geer/. (/tedə/, /tedənər/, and /tedəgeer/ are declined like /edə/, /edənər/, and /edəgeer/, respectively.)

3.423. Pronouns may occur with the possessive suffixes and with the enclitically added short genitive forms of the personal pronouns, see 3.414.

/namaegaa/ 'me of his own'

/nadaaraa/ 'by means of me of his own'

/čamətaegaa/ 'together with thee of his own'

/mantaegaa/ 'together with us of his own'

/tɯɯndəčin/ 'to him of thee'

/tɯɯnteegee/ 'together with him of his own'

/taamin/ 'you of mine'

/bičin/ 'I of thine'

/terəčin/ 'that of thine'

3.43. Verb inflection

The inflection of the verb comprises four main groups of forms:
(1) imperative and voluntative, (2) indicative, (3) verbal
nouns, and (4) gerunds. Most of the forms refer to all three
persons of both numbers.

3.431. Imperative and voluntative

The imperative and voluntative express commands, requests,
wishes, and intentions. They can occur with the negative particles /buш/ and /bitəgii/.

(1) A zero suffix forms an imperative which expresses a
strict order. This form is identical with the stem of the verb.
The prohibitive particle is /bitəgii/ (rarely /buш/).

> /yabə/ 'go!', from /yabə-/
>
> /əg/ 'give!', from /əg-/
>
> /bitəgii yabə/ 'don't go!'

(2) /-gtəŋ/ or /-təŋ/ forms the benedictive, a deferential
or polite request directed to someone who is to be addressed as
/ta/ 'you' (cf. French vous, German Sie) or a group of such persons. The prohibitive particle is usually /bitəgii/.

> /yabəgtəŋ/ or /yabətəŋ/ 'please go!'
>
> /əgəgtəŋ/ or /əgtəŋ/ 'please give!'
>
> /suugtəŋ/ 'please sit down!', from /suu-/
>
> /bitəgii yabəgtəŋ/ 'please don't go!'

(3) /-ee/ forms the so-called precative, a form that indicates humble but urgent begging, which is addressed to the second
person of the singular and plural. In the singular, the pronoun
/či/ 'thou' is added enclitically to the suffix. In the plural,
the pronoun /ta/ 'you' is added. The final vowel of the pronoun
is usually dropped so that the singular form ends in /-eeč/, and
the plural form ends in /-eet/. The prohibitive particle is
usually /bitəgii/.

> /yabaač/ 'go!' (="I implore thee to go")
>
> /əgeeč/ 'give!' (="I implore thee to give")
>
> /əgeet/ 'give!' (="I implore you to give")

(4) /-eeree -өөree -aarae -ooroe/ forms the imperative of
the future, which expresses an order or request which is to be
fulfilled later. The prohibitive particle is /bitəgii/ or
/buɯ/.

> /margaaši yabaarae/ 'go tomorrow!'
>
> /xojim əgөөree/ 'give later!'
>
> /bitəgii yaaraarae/ 'don't hurry!', from /yaarə-/
>   'to hurry'

(5) /-g/ forms the imperative of the third person, which
expresses a grudgingly given permission to perform the action
in question (more or less = "let him do it for all I care").

> /yabəg/ 'let him (them) go!'

(6) /-eesee - өөsee -aasae -oosoe/ expresses a strong but
vain wish for something to happen, a longing for something that
is unlikely to happen. In Khalkha, it refers mainly to the
third person ("if only he ..."), but in other dialects it may
refer also to the first or second person ("if only I ..."; "if
only you ..."). This form is usually called the optative.

> /yabaasae/ 'if only he would go!'
>
> /oroosoe/ 'if only he would enter!'
>
> /uɯxeesee/ 'if only he would die!'

(7) /-yee/ forms the so-called voluntative of the first
person, which expresses the intention to perform the action in
question. The prohibitive particle is usually /buɯ/.

> /yabəyaa/ 'let me go!', 'let us go!'
>
> /əgəyөө/ 'let me give!', 'let us give!'
>
> /suuyaa/ 'let me sit down!', 'let us sit down!'
>
> /buɯ yabəyaa/ 'let us not go!'

(8) In the modern literary language there are several suffixes which have been borrowed from Script Mongolian and are
alien to the colloquial language: -sɯgei/-sugai of the first
person, e.g. /yabəsugae/ 'I will go!'; -tɯgei/-tugai of the third
person, e.g. /mandətəgae/ 'long live!', lit. 'may he rise!'; and
-uɯӡei/-uuӡai, the so-called dubitative, which expresses a fear

that something undesirable may happen, e.g. /oluuʐae/ 'what if he finds it?', from /ol-/ 'to find'.

3.432. Indicative

The indicative forms are finite forms that function as predicates of clauses.

There are four indicative forms. All of them take the interrogative particle /ɯɯ/, and occur, in the modern literary language, with the negative particle /es/, see 3.292.(2). In Colloquial Khalkha the indicative forms do not occur with the negative particles; instead, verbal nouns with following /gɯi/ are used.

(1)   /-nə/ or /-n/ forms the present tense of the imperfect, which denotes a timeless action that may take place in the future or at any indefinite time, e.g. "the train arrives at three o'clock", i.e. every day at the same time.

> /bi medən/ 'I know', from /medə-/ 'to know'
> /či xeʐee irnə/ 'when wilt thou come?', from /ir-/
>   'to come'
> /bagši margaadər irnə/ 'the teacher will come tomorrow'
> /bi es medən/ 'I do not know'

The colloquial equivalent of the phrase /es medən/ 'do not know' is the verbal noun of the future ending in /-xə/ (see 3.433) with the negative particle /gɯi/, e.g. /bi medəxgɯi/ 'I do not know'.

(2)   /-lee/ forms the so-called present tense of the perfect, which expresses an action which has taken place, and which has either been witnessed or is commonly known, and is therefore regarded as an indisputable fact.

> /enee oroe bidə xoyər xamtə guaanʐəndə idəlee/ 'this
>   evening the two of us ate in a restaurant', from
>   /idə-/ 'to eat'
> /bi tanəiig yixə sanəlaa/ 'I have missed you very much',
>   from /sanə-/ 'to think of, to long for'

/bagši irlee/ 'the teacher has come'

/bi es xellee/ 'I did not say'

The colloquial equivalent of the phrase /es xellee/ 'did not say' is the verbal noun of the perfect ending in /-səŋ/ (see 3.433) with the negative particle /gui/, e.g. /xelsəŋgui/ 'did not say', /xelsəŋguyuɯ/ 'didn't he say?'.

(3) /-bə/ or /-b/ forms the so-called past tense of the perfect, which corresponds more or less to the English simple past tense. In statements, it is not often used in the colloquial language, which prefers the verbal noun of the perfect (see 3.433), but in questions it occurs quite frequently with the interrogative particle /uɯ/.

/bosəbə/ or /bosəb/ 'got up', from /bos-/ 'to get up'

/es medəb/ 'did not know'

/ta uʒəbuɯ/ 'did you see?', from /uʒə-/ 'to see'

The colloquial equivalent of the phrase /es medəb/ is the verbal noun of the perfect ending in /-səŋ/ with the negative particle /gui/, e.g. /medəsəŋgui/ 'did not know'.

(4) /-ǰi/ or /-ǰ/ on stems ending in a vowel or /l/, and /-či/ or /-č/ on stems ending in /g d s b r/, forms the so-called past tense of the imperfect, which denotes an action that took place in the past and lasted for some time. In emphatic speech, the suffix is /-ǰee -čee/. It occurs with the negative particles /es/ and /ul/, and with the interrogative particle /uɯ/.

/urgəlǰi undəs tuɯǰi/ 'all the time he collected
    [edible] roots', from /tuɯ-/ 'to collect'

/tiim saeŋ xuɯ baeǰee/ 'there was such a good lad',
    from /bae-/ 'to be'

/nar garči/ 'the sun rose', lit. 'came out', from
    /gar-/ 'to come out'

/bi čamaeg xuleen geǰuɯ/ 'do you mean I am going to
    wait for you?', lit. 'didst thou say I would wait
    for thee?', from /ge-/ 'to say'

/es bolǰee/ 'he did not agree', from /bol-/ 'to agree'

131

The colloquial equivalent of the phrase /es bolǰee/ is the verbal noun of the perfect ending in /-səŋ/ (see 3.433) with the negative particle /gʉi/, e.g. /bolsəŋgʉi/ 'he did not agree'.

3.433. Verbal nouns

Verbal nouns can be derived from all verbs. They possess all features of both nouns and verbs, and may occur with gerunds, whereas the nouns derived from verbs (see 3.313) do not, e.g. /suuǰ uŋšisəŋ/ 'he who read while sitting', i.e. the gerund /suuǰ/ 'sitting' and the verbal noun /uŋšisəŋ/ 'the one who read' (cf. /uŋšilgə/ 'reading', which cannot be preceded by a gerund).

Verbal nouns can be declined and take the plural and possessive suffixes. They function as subjects and predicates of clauses. As predicates, they function as finite verbs, and may occur with the preverbal negative particles /es/ and /ʉl/, or with the negative particle /gʉi/ which is added to nouns. They also take the interrogative particles /ʉʉ/ and /bə/ ~ /b/; see 3.291.

(1) /-gči/ forms the verbal noun of the actor. It functions as a noun or adjective or verb. As a noun, it is declinable, takes the plural suffix /+d/, and the possessive suffixes. As a verb, it takes the negative particle /es/.

/yabəgči/ 'goer, going'

/uŋšigči/ 'reader, reading'

/erxəm uŋšigči/ 'esteemed reader!'

/erxəm uŋšigčid/ 'esteemed readers!'

/uŋšigči xʉʉxəŋ/ 'the reading girl, the girl who reads'

/temtərč sudləgči/ 'one who examines by groping', from /sudlə-/ 'to examine'

/taanər tusləgči baetəgae namaeg xuurdəg imaa/ 'you are not only not helping but you always deceive me!', from /tuslə-/ 'to help'

/es medəgči bolbə/ 'he pretended not to know', lit. 'he became a not-knowing-one'

(2) /-ee/, after geminate vowel phonemes or diphthongs /-gee/, forms the noun of the imperfect, which functions as a noun, adjective, or verb, denoting actions that began in the past and are still continuing at the time of speaking.

/gaexəǰ sonirxəǰ suugaan či bidə xoyər/ 'those who
sit, marvelling and interested, are the two of us',
lit. 'marvelling and being interested the sitting
ones are thou, we, two', from /suu-/ 'to sit' with
the possessive suffix /+n/ of the third person.

/ardəčin yabaa bɯsgɯi/ 'the woman walking behind
thee'

/minii xɯɯ cerəgtə dargaar baegaa/ 'my son has been
an officer in the army', lit. 'my son has been in
the capacity of an officer in the army'

/ta xaraa biiʒə/ 'you have probably seen', from /xarə-/
'to see'

/galtə ireeyɯɯ/ 'has Galta come?'

/či xaečiǰ yabaabə/ 'where art thou going?', from
/yabə-/ 'to walk, to go' with the interrogative
particle /bə/

/galtə ireegɯi/ 'Galta has not come'

(3) /-səŋ/ (stem /-sən+/) forms the verbal noun of the perfect, which denotes completed (finished) actions that took place in the past. It functions as subject, predicate, attribute, and, with case suffixes, as complement. As a predicate, with or without a copula, it functions as the past tense, and in Colloquial Khalkha, it is preferred to the past tense in /-bə/.

/yabəsənin irlee/ 'he who was gone has come', lit.
'the gone one has come'

/yabəsəd irlee/ 'those who had gone have come' (plural
of /yabəsəŋ/)

/martəsənəiig sanuulxə/ 'to remind of what has been
forgotten', acc. of /martəsəŋ/ 'the forgotten one',
from /martə-/ 'to forget'

/uulʒəsəŋ nexər/ 'the comrade who has been met', from
/uulʒə-/ 'to meet'

/cerəŋ ičisəndee uilsəŋ/ 'when he was ashamed, Tseren
cried', lit. 'in his own being ashamed, Tseren
cried', from /iči-/ 'to be ashamed', dat.-loc. with
the reflexive possessive suffix

/batə surguuliaa təgəssəŋ/ 'Bata has graduated from
school', from /təgəs-/ 'to finish, to complete'

/batə irsəŋɯi/ 'Bata did not come'

/batə irsəŋɯyɯɯ/ 'didn't Bata come?'

/batə xeʒee irsəmbə/ 'when did Bata come?', from
/irsəŋ/ plus /bə/

(4) /-dəg/ forms a verbal noun indicating a habitually or
frequently performed action. It functions as subject, predicate,
attribute, and complement.

/eejiiŋ xeldəg ʒeb dee/ 'what mother usually says is,
indeed, true'

/xeldəg gurbə, xiidəg gancə/ 'those who talk all the
time are three [but] he who [really] does [some-
thing] is only one', lit. 'constant talkers are
three, and doer is only one', from /xel-/ 'to say,
speak, talk' and /xii-/ 'to do'

/duɯn sonsədəg/ 'his younger brother always listens',
from /sonsə-/ 'to listen'

/činii abčirdəgiig bi abənə šɯɯ/ 'I certainly take
what you always bring', lit. 'don't I take thy
always brought?', from /abčir-/ 'to bring'

/altəŋ gurgəldae alinaasč ilɯɯ doŋgədədəg/ 'the
nightingale usually sings better than anything',
from /doŋgədə-/ 'to twitter, to sing'

/taanərəiiŋ sedxəl amərdəguu/ 'is your mind usually
at peace?', from /amər-/ 'to be peaceful, to be at
peace'

(5) /-xə/ forms a verbal noun which denotes an action
which will be performed in the future. It functions as any

member of a clause. As a predicate, with the negative particle
/gɯi/, it is the negative counterpart of the present tense.
This verbal noun is often translated as an infinitive, and in
most dictionaries the verbs are given in this form.

> /nar garxə oertəbə/ 'sunrise was near', lit. 'the
>   sun's coming out approached'
>
> /irxə ǰil/ 'next year', lit. 'the year which will
>   come'
>
> /batə udəxəgɯi irxə yɯm/ 'Bata will come soon', lit.
>   'Bata will come without being late', from /udə-/
>   'to last long, to be late' and /ir-/ 'to come' with
>   the copula /yɯm/
>
> /bucəxəiig yaarnə/ 'he hurries to go back', from
>   /bucə-/ 'to return, to go back' with the acc. suf-
>   fix.
>
> /bi irxəgɯi/ 'I shall not come'

3.434. Gerunds

Gerunds (or converbs) function as verbal modifiers or adverbial
complements, and denote actions which accompany the action of
the main verb, or the circumstances under which the action of
the finite verb takes place. Some gerunds occur with the negative particle /es/ or /ɯl/, but most of them do not occur with
negative particles at all: instead, special phrases are used
(see 3.4341). Some gerunds take the possessive suffixes and the
short genitive forms of the pronouns, and some occur with the
interrogative particle /ɯɯ/.

   (1) /-ŋ/ forms the so-called modal gerund. When immediately preceding the main verb, it indicates the manner in which
the main action is carried out, e.g. /nisəŋ ir-/ 'to fly to',
lit. 'to come flying'; /bi xašxirəŋ xelbə/ 'I shouted [to him
the following words]', lit. 'I said shouting', from /xašxirə-/
'to shout'.

   When separated from the main verb by other words, this
gerund expresses an action simultaneous with that of the main

verb, e.g. /tɯɯnii uur xiləŋ ɯrgəlǰi badərəŋ durgɯicəxən uləm nemǝgdǝsǝŋ/ 'his anger constantly growing, his dislike grev still more', from /badərǝ-/ 'to grow, to expand'.

When repeated, this gerund expresses a frequently repeated action, e.g. /xarəŋ xarəŋ uilǝnǝ/ 'he weeps, glancing all the time [at him]', lit. 'looking looking, weeps', from /xarǝ-/ 'to look'.

(2) /-ǰi/ or /-ǰ/ after a stem-final vowel or /l/, /-či/ or /-č/ after a stem-final /g d b s r/, forms the imperfect gerund, otherwise called the gerund of the simultaneous action, which expresses an action that takes place simultaneously with the action of the main verb.

> /nar xelbiiǰ oroeŋ serɯɯŋ amisgəl orǝbǝ/ 'the sun
>   sinking, the evening's cool breeze began', from
>   /xelbii-/ 'to incline'
> /moritoe xɯŋ irǰ buubǝ/ 'a horseman came and dis-
>   mounted', lit. 'coming, dismounted'

The imperfect gerund functions also as a verbal complement in expressions such as /nom ɯʒəǰ exəlsəŋ/ 'he began to read', from /ɯʒǝ-/ 'to read'; /uŋšiǰi čadǝnǝ/ 'he can read', from /uŋši-/ 'to read'; /uŋšiǰi sursǝŋ/ 'he learned to read'.

The imperfect gerund followed by /baenǝ/ 'is' functions as the English progressive present, e.g. /uŋšiǰi baenǝ/ 'is reading'.

(3) /-eed/, after geminate vowels or diphthongs /-geed/, forms the gerund of the perfect, which denotes an action which precedes, in time, that of the main verb. It occurs with the negative particle /es/, and with the interrogative particle /ɯɯ/.

> /iŋgəǰ asuugaad xəmsǝgee atiruulbǝ/ 'having asked so,
>   he frowned', from /asuu-/ 'to ask'
> /iŋgəǰi ʒogsooduu/ 'having thus stopped?', from
>   /ʒogsǝ-/ 'to stop'
> /es olood gaexǝsaar baeb/ 'not having found [it], he
>   stood wondering', from /ol-/ 'to find'

/ǰabər namdaad cas orǰ exələb/ 'the wind having de-
creased, snow began to fall', from /namdə-/ 'to
decrease, to fall, to become low'

/saeŋ yabaad ireeree/ 'have a nice trip and come
[back well]!', lit. 'having gone well, come [back]!'

(4) /-bəl/ forms the conditional gerund, which denotes an
action which constitutes the condition for another action. This
gerund occurs with the negative particle /es/.

Colloquial Khalkha prefers, however, a phrase consisting of
a verbal noun and the conditional gerund of /bol-/ 'to become',
i.e. /bolbəl/, which is often shortened to /bol/ or /bəl/.

/uul xerəb daerəldəbəl dabaad bidə garnə/ 'if a
mountain is encountered, we will go across it',
lit. 'if a mountain is met, we, having gone over
[it], shall come out', from /daerəldə-/ 'to meet
each other, to run across each other'

/bodəbəl tarni uŋšiǰ baexə boləltoe/ 'if one thinks
[about it], he seems to be reading a magic formula',
from /bodə-/ 'to think'

/bidə togləŋ asuubəl dulmaa xelsənin/ '[this is] what
Dulmaa said when we asked [her] jokingly]', from
/asuu-/ 'to ask'

/axəčin əčigdər irsəŋ bol/ 'if your elder brother came
yesterday ...'

/či margaadər irxə bol/ 'if thou comest tomorrow ...'

/ta es irəbəl/ 'if you do not come ...'

/ta irxəgɯi bolbəl/ or /ta irxəgɯi bol/ 'if you do not
come ...'

(5) /-bəč/ forms the concessive gerund, which denotes an
action in spite of which another action takes place (or does not
take place). Colloquial Khalkha prefers, however, a verbal noun
with the particle /č/, see 3.293.

/batə irbəč cecegee yabənə/ 'although Bata comes,
Tsetsegei goes'

/ʋndər uulən+deerees šīrtəbəč xoləiiŋ baraa xarəgdəxguɪi/
'although one looks attentively from the top of a high
mountain, the outlines of distant [objects] are not
seen', from /šīrtə-/ 'to fix one's gaze on something'

/yaaǰ bodəbəč neriin oləx yuɪm biš/ 'no matter how [much]
I think, [I] cannot remember his name', from /bodə-/
'to think'

/irsənč tusguɪi baenə/ 'although he has come, it is of no
use'

(6) /-seer/ forms the so-called abtemporal gerund, which
denotes an action since the time of which another action has
taken place, or a continuous and lasting action.

/xuučiŋ xuɪuɪ xul morin+deer xəndləŋ suuǰ xatiruulsaar
xuɪrč irbə/ 'Khuuchin Khuu, sitting on a bay horse,
arrived, while continuously making [his horse] trot',
from /xatiruul-/ 'to cause to trot'

/xoosəŋ xubiŋgaa xaŋginuulsaar orǰ irbə/ 'he entered
while clanking his empty bucket', from /xaŋginuul-/
'to clank, to cause to make noise'

/bi irseer gurbə xonəǰ baenə/ 'it is three days since
I came', lit. 'I am spending three days and nights
since I came'

(7) /-xleer/ forms the successive gerund, which denotes an
action which is followed immediately by another action. This
gerund occurs with the possessive suffixes and the short genitive
forms of the pronouns.

/yabəxlaaraa xeleeree/ 'as soon as you go, tell [about
it]!', from /yabə-/ 'to go', with the reflexive
possessive suffix

/irxleerčin uulʒənə/ 'as soon as thou comest, [we]
shall meet', from /ir-/ 'to come', with /čin/ 'thy'

(8) /-məgcə/ forms the so-called contemporal gerund, which
denotes an action which is immediately joined by the action of
the main verb. This gerund occurs with the possessive suffixes
and the short genitive forms of the pronouns.

/čuluuŋ nom uŋšiməgcaa bɯxə yuməiig martədəg baejee/
'Chuluun used to forget everything the moment he
read the book', from /uŋši-/ 'to read', with the
reflexive possessive suffix

/bi očiməgcoo čamdə ʒaxiaa bičinə/ 'I shall write thee
a letter the moment I go', from /oči-/ 'to go away',
with the reflexive possessive suffix

/duu exəlməgcəmin či dagəj duulaarae/ 'the moment I
start singing, thou sing also!', lit. 'the moment
I begin the song, thou sing following [me]!', from
/exəl-/ 'to begin'

(9) /-təl/, in dialects also /-tər/, forms the so-called
terminal gerund, which denotes an action until which that of the
main verb lasts, or an action which is the measure of that of
the main verb, or an action during which that of the main verb
takes place. This gerund occurs with the possessive suffixes
and the short genitive forms of the pronouns.

/namaeg irtəl xɯleej bae/ 'wait until I come!'

/batə xinoo ɯʒətəlee xičeel dabtəj suujee/ 'Bata sat
repeating his home work until he saw the movie',
from /ɯʒə-/ 'to see', with the reflexive possessive
suffix

/surguuli cuglətəl xədee amərč baegaa/ 'he is resting
in the countryside until school starts', from /cuglə-/
'to assemble'

/xuurae modəiig xugərtəl ʒodood baejee/ 'they beat him
so that the dry stick broke', from /xugər-/ 'to
break'

/guaanʒəndə orood negə suudəl olood suutəl xool ʒeegči
irlee/ '[we] entered the restaurant and found a seat,
and while [we] sat the waiter came', from /suu-/ 'to
sit'

The terminal gerund with the ablative case has a concessive
meaning.

139

/saeŋ xɯŋ baetəlaas sanaa ɯgɯi/ 'although [you] are a
fine man, [you] are thoughtless'

(10) /-ŋgee/ forms a gerund which denotes an action performed in passing, so to speak, and requiring no special effort
or time for its performance.

/či xotə orəŋgoo manae dɯɯgiiŋxeer orood ireeree/
'come [back] having called, on your way to town, on
our younger brother!', lit. 'entering the town,
come [back] having called on our younger brother!',
from /or-/ 'to enter'

3.4341. In Colloquial Khalkha, and in some other dialects, the
gerunds do not occur with the negative particles. Instead,
special phrases are used which consist of the verb /bae-/ (in
some cases /bol-/) in the gerund form in question preceded by a
verbal noun (usually in /-xə/ or /-səŋ/) with the negative
particle, e.g. /yabəxəgɯi baeǰi/ 'not going'.

Following are the gerunds and the corresponding negative
forms:

(1) Modal /-ŋ/ : /yabəŋ/ 'walking' : /yabəlgɯi/ 'not
walking'

(2) Imperfect /-ǰ/ : /yabəǰ/ 'walking' : /yabəxəgɯi baeǰ/
'not walking'

(3) Perfect /-eed/ : /yabaad/ 'having walked' : /yabəxəgɯi
baegaad/ 'having not walked'

(4) Conditional /-bəl/ : /yabəbəl/ 'if he goes' : /yabəxəgɯi
bol/ 'if he does not go'

(5) Concessive /-bəč/ : /yabəbəč/ 'although he goes' :
/yabəxəgɯi bolbəč/ 'although he does not go'

(6) Abtemporal /-seer/ : /yabəsaar/ 'since he went' :
/yabəxəgɯi bolsoor/ 'since he did not go'

(7) Successive /-xleer/ : /yabəxlaar/ 'as soon as he went' :
/yabəxəgɯi bolxəloor/ 'as soon as he did not go'

(8) Contemporal /-məgcə/ : /yabəməgcə/ 'the moment he went' :
/yabəxəgɯi bolməgcə/ 'the moment he would not go'

(9)   Terminal /-təl/ : /yabətəl/ 'until he went' :

/yabaxəgɯi baetəl/ 'until he did not go'

(10) The gerund in /-ŋgee/ does not occur in negative

phrases.

3.5. Select bibliography

Orčin cagiǐn mongol xèl züǐ, BNMAU Sinžlèx uxaani akademi, Ulaan Baatar, 1966.

Poppe, N., Khalkha-mongolische Grammatik, Mit Bibliographie, Sprachproben und Glossar, Wiesbaden, 1951.

-----, "Die Nominalstammbildungssuffixe im Mongolischen", Keleti Szemle XX, 1923-27, pp. 89-126.

Ramstedt, G.J., Über die Konjugation des Khalkha-Mongolischen (Mémoires de la Société Finno-Ougrienne XIX), Helsinki, 1903.

-----, "Zur Verbstammbildungslehre der mongolisch-türkischen Sprachen", Journal de la Société Finno-Ougrienne XXVIII:2 (1912), pp. 1-86.

Street, John S., Khalkha Structure (Uralic and Altaic Series, vol. 24), Bloomington, Indiana, 1963.

4. SYNTAX

4.1. Phrase-structure

4.10. Phrase

A phrase is a group of words which constitutes a part of a
clause and functions as a given word-category. Thus, in the
clause /xɯŋ bɯr saeŋ ajillǝxǝ xerǝgtee/ 'everybody must work
well' the word groups /xɯŋ bɯr/ 'everybody' (lit. 'every person'), /ajillǝxǝ xerǝgtee/ 'must work' (lit. 'with the working
necessity'), and /saeŋ ajillǝxǝ/ 'well working', are phrases.

The head of a phrase may be a single word or another
phrase.

There are two types of phrases, namely, co-ordinate phrases
and contrastive phrases.

4.101. Co-ordinate phrases

Co-ordinate phrases have two or more heads of like function.
Declension suffixes are normally added only to the last head,
e.g. /modǝ čuluugaar/ 'by means of wood and stone'. In cases
in which the heads are compound nouns, a declension suffix is
added to each head, e.g. /aabijiidee axǝdɯɯnǝrtee/ 'to his own
parents (lit. 'father, mother') [and] to his own brothers (lit.
'to his own elder, younger brothers')'.

Co-ordinate phrases are of two types, namely, without conjunctions and with conjunctions.

4.1011. Co-ordinate phrases without conjunctions consist of two
or more heads juxtaposed, e.g. /ajilčiŋ oyuutǝŋ bagšinǝr
bɯgǝdeeree sanǝl negǝtee demjij baenǝ/ 'the workers, the students, the teachers, all of them are helping unanimously'.

4.1012. Co-ordinate phrases with conjunctions are of two types.

(1) Phrases consisting of two or more heads, the last of which is preceded by a conjunction, e.g. /xoni ba yamaanəii noos/ 'wool of sheep and goats'; /albəŋ ɯilədbəriiŋ boləŋ xədəlmərčidiiŋ orəŋ baerəiiŋ ariuuŋ cebəriig saejiruulxə/ 'to improve the cleanness and tidiness of state-owned industrial buildings and of workers' living quarters'.

(2) Phrases consisting of two or more heads, the last of which is followed by a summarizing numeral indicating the total number of objects in question, the numeral also taking the declensional suffix, e.g. /xoni yamaa xoyər/ 'the sheep and the goat' (lit. 'sheep, goat, two'); /tuulae teləg čonə gurbəiig/ 'the hare, the lamb, and the wolf' (lit. 'the hare, lamb, wolf, three').

4.102. Contrastive phrases

Contrastive phrases consist of two heads, the second of which is preceded by a contrastive conjunction, e.g. /čonə biši xariŋ negə noxoe/ 'not a wolf but a dog'.

A contrastive conjunction may be omitted when the first head is followed by the negative particle /biši/, e.g. /saeŋ biši muu/ 'not good [but] bad'.

4.11. Nominal phrases

Nominal phrases have as their head a noun or any word that functions as a noun.

4.111. Attribute + head

(1) Nouns may act as attributes, either functioning as adjectives or denoting a measure. Proper names act as attributes of names of professions, rivers, cities, etc.

/xɯɯxəŋ dɯɯ/ 'younger sister': /xɯɯxəŋ/ 'girl',
/dɯɯ/ 'younger sibling'
/arbəŋ xəxɯɯr arxi/ 'ten wineskins of liquor':

/arbəŋ/ 'ten', /xəxɯɯr/ 'wineskin', /arxi/ 'alcohol
or kind of vodka made of milk'

/ulaambaatər xotə/ 'the city of Ulan Bator'

/orxəŋ mərəŋ/ 'the Orkhon River'

/xɯŋ bɯgədə/ 'all people': /xɯŋ/ 'man, person',
/bɯgədə/ 'total number'

An attribute in the genitive denotes the possessor of something or an object to which something belongs.

/bagšiiŋ nom/ 'the book of the teacher': /bagšiiŋ/
gen. of /bagši/ 'teacher'

/aabəiiŋ ger/ 'the yurt of the father': /aabəiiŋ/
gen. of /aabə/ 'father'

/gobiiŋ čonə/ 'a Gobi wolf': /gobiiŋ/ gen. of /gobi/
'sandy steppe with sparse vegetation'

/tɯiməriiŋ utaa/ 'the smoke of the fire': /tɯiməriiŋ/
gen. of /tɯimər/ 'fire, conflagration'

/uliaastaeŋ gol/ 'the Uliasutai River'

/beejiŋgiiŋ xotə/ 'the city of Peking': /beejiŋ+/
'Peking'

(2) The attribute is an adjective or a word functioning
as an adjective. The adjective may be an interrogative adjective, a numeral, or an adjective denoting a quantity.

/yamər xɯŋ/ 'what kind of a person?': /yamər/ 'what,
what kind of'

/saeŋ mori/ 'a good horse': /saeŋ/ 'good'

/gurbəŋ xɯŋ/ 'three persons': /gurbəŋ/ 'three'

/oləŋ xɯŋ/ 'many persons': /oləŋ/ 'many'

(3) The attribute is a demonstrative pronoun. A plural
demonstrative pronoun may refer to a singular noun, in which
event the noun has the meaning of a plural.

/edə nəxəd/ 'these comrades': /edə/ 'these'

/edəgeer noməiig uŋšibə/ '[he] read these books':
/edəgeer/ 'these', /noməiig/ acc. of /nom/ 'book'

(4) The attribute may be a verbal noun which functions as
an adjective.

/irəsəŋ xɯŋ/ 'a person who has come'

/irəxə ǰil/ 'the coming year'

/ɯxəsəŋ xɯŋ/ 'a dead person': /ɯxəsəŋ/ 'who has died',
from /ɯxə-/ 'to die'

A.   The verbal noun may be preceded by a gerund or a
complement.

/uŋšiǰ suusəŋ xɯŋ/ 'a person who was sitting and
reading' (lit. 'a person who sat reading')

/xool belədxəsəŋ xɯŋ/ 'a person who has prepared
food': /belədxəsəŋ/, from /belədxə-/ 'to prepare'

/gertə orəsəŋ xɯŋ/ 'a person who entered the yurt':
/orəsəŋ/, from /orə-/ 'to enter'; /gertə/ dat. of
/ger/ 'yurt'

B.   The actor of a verbal noun of an intransitive verb
is usually in the subject-direct object form.

/xɯŋ suusəŋ gaʒər/ 'a place where a person sat' (lit.
'a person-having-sat place')

C.   The actor of a verbal noun of a transitive verb
is usually in the genitive form.

/bagšiiŋ bičisəŋ ʒaxidal/ 'a letter written by the
teacher'

/minii acərsəŋ nom/ 'a book brought by me': /acərsəŋ/
'brought' from /acər-/ 'to bring'

D.   A special case is an adjectival phrase consisting
of a noun, usually with the possessive suffix of the third
person, and an adjective (or verbal noun). Considered
separately, the phrase is a clause in which the noun is the
subject and the adjective (or verbal noun) is the predicate.

/deelən tos bolsəŋ xɯŋ/ 'a man whose coat was soiled
with grease' (lit. 'a his-coat-has-become-grease man')

4.112. Several attributes

A noun may have more than one attribute, in which case they occur
in the following order:

(1) The adjective is closest to the head, the numeral preceding it, e.g. /gurbəŋ xarə mori/ 'three black horses'.

(2) A demonstrative pronoun usually precedes all the other attributes, e.g. /terə soniŋ nom/ 'that interesting book'.

(3) Words indicating permanent characteristics of an object are closest to the head, e.g. /xegšiŋ xarə mori/ 'the old black horse'; /ulaaŋ modəŋ baešiŋ/ 'a red wooden house'; /ulaaŋ torgəŋ deel/ 'a red silken coat'.

(4) A genitive attribute usually precedes the other attributes, e.g. /aabəiiŋ šinə nom/ 'the new book of the father'; /aabəiiŋ gurbəŋ xarə mori/ 'three black horses of the father'.

(5) Sometimes a numeral may precede the genitive attribute even though it refers to the head, e.g. /tuməŋ narnəii tuyaa/ 'ten thousands of sunbeams'.

4.12. Adjectival phrases

(1) The head is an adjective, and when substantivized has the possessive suffix of the third person. The attribute is a noun in the genitive. Such phrases function as superlatives.

> /unəgənii ulaaŋ/ 'the reddest of foxes' (lit. 'of the
>   fox[es] red': /unəgən+/ 'fox', /ulaaŋ/ 'red')
> /eriiŋ saeŋ/ 'the best of the men': /eriiŋ/ gen. of
>   /erə/ 'man', /saeŋ/ 'good'
> /xamgiiŋ saenin/ 'the best of all': /xamgiiŋ/ gen. of
>   /xaməg/ 'all', /saen+/ 'good', with the poss. suff.

(2) An adjective preceded by a noun in the ablative has the meaning of the comparative.

> /temeenees əndər/ 'higher than a camel': /temeenees/
>   abl. of /temeen+/ 'camel'
> /altənaas unətee/ 'more expensive than gold': /altənaas/
>   abl. of /altən+/ 'gold', /unətee/ 'dear, expensive'

(3) An adjective may be preceded by the nominative form of a noun, which in its turn is preceded by a numeral.

> /gurbəŋ aldə urtə/ 'three fathoms long': /aldə/
>   'fathom', /urtə/ 'long'

(4) An adjective may be preceded by another adjective or a word which functions as an adjective. In such phrases the first adjective modifies the second adjective.

/ulaaŋ ʒeerdə/ 'red chestnut-colored': /ulaaŋ/ 'red',
/ʒeerdə/ 'chestnut' (horse)

/xeer baraaŋ/ 'dark bay': /xeer/ 'bay', /baraan/ 'dark'

(5) An adjective may be preceded by an adverb or a word which functions adverbially.

/maši saeŋ/ 'very good'

/malaar bayəŋ/ 'rich in cattle': /malaar/ instr. of
/mal/ 'cattle'

/moŋgəl xeləndə saeŋ/ 'good in the Mongolian language',
i.e. knowing Mongolian well: /xeləndə/ dat. of
/xelən+/ ~ /xel+/ 'language'

4.13. Adverbial phrases

A noun in a case form other than the subject-direct object form may function adverbially.

An adverb may function as attribute, and an adverb may also have an attribute.

(1) Adverb as attribute, e.g. /maši saeŋ/ 'very good';
/denduш xolə/ 'too far'.

(2) Adjective functioning adverbially, e.g. /yixə saeŋ/
'very good': /yixə/ 'great, large', /saeŋ/ 'good'.

(3) Adverb with a pronoun as attribute, e.g. /manae endə/
'here at us' (lit. 'our here').

4.14. Postpositional phrases

(1) A noun, pronoun, or another substantivized part of speech with a postposition, e.g. /aǰiləiiŋ tul/ 'because of work'; /surguuliiŋ tuxae/ 'about the school'; /tuшnii telee/ 'for the sake of that'; /irsənii tul/ 'because of coming', a verbal noun with a postposition.

(2) The same parts of speech followed by a noun functioning as a postposition, e.g. /geriiŋ xaǰuudə/ 'by the yurt':
/xaǰuudə/ dat. of /xaǰuu/ 'side'.

(3) An adverb followed by a postposition, e.g. /endə
xɯrtəl/ 'until here'.

4.15. Verbal phrases

Verbal phrases consist of a verb preceded by one or more complements.

4.151. Equational complement

(1) The equational complement is a noun, pronoun, or
adjective in the subject-direct object form, followed by a
copula which may, however, be omitted.

The copula is a finite form of the verbs /bae-/ 'to be'
and /bol-/ 'to become', or /yum/ 'is' or /mən/ 'is indeed' (in
emphatic speech).

> /enə nom soniŋ baenə/ 'this book is interesting'
> /dorǰi bagši baesəŋ/ 'Dorji was a teacher'
> /bi bagši baenə/ 'I am a teacher'
> /manae xɯɯ bagši bolnə/ 'our son will become a teacher'
> /enə xerəg xecɯɯ yum/ 'this affair is difficult'
> /terə saeŋ yum+seŋ/ 'that was good'
> /dorǰi manae erxələgči məŋ/ 'Dorji is indeed our
> manager'
> /dorǰi saeŋ erxələgči məŋ/ 'Dorji is indeed a good
> manager'

(2) The equational complement is a noun or pronoun in the
genitive. Such verbal phrases indicate that the subject belongs
to what is denoted by the equational complement, e.g. /terə nom
minii baenə/ 'that book is mine'.

4.152. Direct object complement

The direct object is a noun, pronoun, or any substantivized
part of speech, including verbal nouns. The direct object complement indicates the goal of an action, i.e. an object directly
affected by the action. The complement is either a subject-
direct object form or an accusative form.

(1) Pronouns, substantivized adjectives, numerals, verbal nouns, and phrases are always accusative forms (with or without a possessive suffix or a short genitive form of a personal pronoun).

>/namaeg duudəsəŋ/ '[he] called me'
>
>/xcdəŋ saenəiig ɯldeed abči/ 'he spared several good ones and took [them]'
>
>/arbəiig neməsəŋ/ '[he] added ten'
>
>/gurbuuləiig duudəsəŋ/ 'he called all three of them'
>
>/suuǰ baexəiig ɯʒəbə/ 'he saw the sitting one'
>
>/tɯɯniig suuǰ baexəiig ɯʒəbə/ 'he saw him sit'

(2) Proper nouns and nouns denoting people always appear in the accusative, e.g. /dorǰiig duudə/ 'call Dorji!'; /bagšiig ʒaləbə/ 'he invited the teacher'.

(3) Nouns having a possessive attribute (genitive of a personal pronoun or noun denoting a person), nouns with a possessive suffix, or nouns followed by a short genitive form of a personal pronoun are always in the accusative form.

>/moriičin unəlaa/ '[he] rode thy horse'
>
>/bi axəiiŋxaa xaalgəiig ʒasəbə/ 'I have repaired my elder brother's gate'
>
>/bi xaalgəiin ʒasəbə/ 'I have repaired his gate'
>
>/bi činii moriig unəyaa/ 'let me ride thy horse'

(4) All other nouns appear in the subject-direct object form when immediately followed by the governing verb. When separated by other words from the verb, they appear in the accusative form.

>/ʒurəg ʒurəbə/ '[he] painted a picture'
>
>/ʒurəgiig urəŋ ʒurəgči čoedəg ʒurǰee/ 'the painter Choidog painted the picture'
>
>/šinə barilgə baribə/ '[he] built a new building'
>
>/šinə barilgəiig nutəgiiŋ arəduud baribə/ 'the local people built a new building'

4.153. <u>Adverbial complement</u>

Adverbs, adjectives, numerals, nouns and pronouns in various case forms (including the subject-direct object form), nouns or pronouns with a postposition, verbal noun phrases, gerunds, and gerundial phrases may act as adverbial complements.

(1) Adverb with or without a possessive suffix, e:g. /gentə toxiooldəbə/ '[it] happened suddenly'; /xugə coxibə/ '[he] broke [it] in two'; /urəgšaa yabəbə/ '[he] went forward': /urəgši/ 'forward', with the reflexive possessive suffix; /xoešin tabi/ 'put it in the back!': /xoeši/ 'backwards', with the possessive suffix of the third person.

(2) Adjective, e.g. /saeŋ medənə/ '[he] knows well'; /erteer bosəbə/ '[he] rose early': /erteer/ instr. of /ertə/ 'early'.

(3) Numeral, e.g. /gurbə balgəǰi/ '[he] gulped down three times': /gurbə/ 'three'.

(4) Noun or pronoun, e.g. /gurbəŋ udaa irəbə/ '[he] came three times'; /ta xotə ornuu/ 'will you enter town?'; /morioor irəbə/ '[he] came by horse'; /irxə ǰildə irənə/ '[he] will come next year'; /tɯɯgeer yɯɯxiixəbə/ 'what do [they] do with that?], instr. of /terə/ 'that'; /ta dorǰišig xičeelee dabtəǰ bae/ '(you) repeat your lesson like Dorji!'; /činii tul iim xerəg xiibə/ '[he] did such a thing because of thee'.

(5) Verbal noun phrase. The verbal noun usually takes a personal possessive suffix (when the actor of the phrase is different from the subject of the clause) or a reflexive possessive suffix (when the actor of the phrase is identical with the subject of the clause). When the actor of a verbal phrase is different from the subject of the clause, the word denoting the actor is usually in the genitive or the accusative.

> /sɯndəryaagiiŋ yarixədə sɯrəŋ uləm bayərləŋ asuubə/
> 'when Sunderyaa talked, Suren asked still more
> happily' (the actor is in the genitive); /sɯndəryaag
> xoninəiixoo xoenoos yabəxədə sɯrəŋ bucəjee/ 'when
> Sunderyaa went after her sheep, Suren went back'

/arbəŋ modəiig suːxeer coxixədə ʒuuŋ modə gaʒəraas
urgənə/ 'when he cuts with the ax ten trees,
[another] one hundred trees grow from the ground'
/morioo unaad dabxixədə manae cog ʒali sergənə/
'when [we] gallop, riding our horses, our grandeur
awakens'

(6) Gerund with or without a negative particle, e.g.
/unšij suunə/ '[he] sits reading'; /nisəŋ irəbə/ '[he] came
flying'; /es medəj orəbə/ 'not knowing (or unknowingly), [he]
entered'.

(7) Gerund with a preceding verbal noun and negative
particle, e.g. /yabəxəguːi baej nileeŋ udəsəŋ/ 'not going, he
lingered [there] considerably'.

(8) Gerundial phrases, except for the gerunds ending in
/-j/, /-ŋ/, and /-eed/, when the actor is different from the
subject of the clause, have the actor in the accusative or
genitive form. Some gerunds take the possessive suffixes and
the short genitive forms of personal pronouns. When the actor
of the gerundial phrase is identical with the subject of the
clause, the gerund takes the reflexive possessive suffix. In
cases in which the actor of the gerundial phrase is different
from the subject of the clause, the gerund takes the personal
possessive suffix of the third person or a short genitive form
of a personal pronoun.

/tuːməŋ suːrəg bilčij aeluːudəiiŋ gerees utaa manərnə/
'ten thousands of herds grazing, smoke rises from
the yurts of the neighborhood'
/xoosəŋ xubiŋgaa xaŋginuulsaar orj irəbə/ 'he entered
while rattling his empty bucket'
/ecəgiini irətəl xuːleej bolxguːyuːuː/ 'is it not possible
to wait until his father comes?'
/čamaeg amidə yabəbəl negə učir bii/ 'there is a
reason [for it] if you are [still] alive'
/yabəxlaaraa xeleeree/ 'tell [him] as soon as you go!'
/uŋsixlaarin sonsooroe/ 'listen the moment he starts
reading!'

151

4.2. Clause-structure

4.20. Clause

A clause may consist of one or more words or phrases, e.g. /suu/ 'sit down!'; /saeŋ yabaarae/ 'bon voyage!' (lit. 'go well!'); /ta bagši mənɯɯ/ 'are you the teacher?'. Mongolian does not have compound clauses of the English type. Clauses are classified as full or minor.

4.21. Full clauses

Full clauses have as their basic element the predicate, which may or may not have a subject, e.g. /irəyee/ '[I] will come'; /xɯŋ irəsəŋ/ 'somebody has come' (lit. 'a person has come').

4.211. The predicate

The predicate has as its center any of the following word-categories.

(1) A verb or equivalent phrase.

/ertə urdə negə tomə ẓaaŋ baeǰi/ 'once upon a time (lit. 'early and formerly') [there] was a large elephant'

/manae dɯɯ surguulidə ornə/ 'our younger brother will enter school'

/bayərtə xičeelee dabtəǰ baebə/ 'Bayarta was repeating his lesson'

(2) A noun, adjective, pronoun, or verbal noun.

A. With a copula:

/manae bagši terə baenə/ 'our teacher is that one'

/enə nom soniŋ yum/ 'this book is interesting'

/bayəŋ boldəiiŋ nasən dečeed baenə/ 'Bayan Bolod's age is approximately forty'

/egəči yabəčisəŋ baelaa/ 'the elder sister was gone'

B. Without a copula:

/manae xɯɯ bagši/ 'our son [is] a teacher'

/manae bagši terə/ 'our teacher [is] that one'

/saeŋ xɯndə nəxər oləŋ/ 'a good person has many
friends' (lit. 'to a good person, the friends [are]
many')

/əčigdəriiŋ temceendə tɯrɯɯlsəŋ xɯŋ terə/ 'the man
who was the first in yesterday's competition [is] he'

/bars enə ǰil naemətae/ 'this year Bars [will be]
eight'

/enə noməiig bi xedəŋ ǰiliiŋ urdə uŋšisəŋ/ 'I read this
book several years ago'

4.2111. A predicate is modified by an adverb, adjective, or gerund.
A verbal predicate, including a verbal noun, is modified by a
gerund. A noun functioning as a predicate is modified by an
adjective. An adjective functioning as a predicate is modified
by an adverb.

/manae xɯɯ saeŋ bagši baenə/ 'our son is a good teacher'

/enə nom maši soniŋ/ 'this book [is] very interesting'

/terə xɯŋ yariǰi suunə/ 'that man sits talking'

4.212. The subject

The subject is either a noun, a pronoun, a substantivized adjective, a numeral, a verbal noun, or a phrase. A personal or
demonstrative pronoun functioning as subject is always in the
nominative. All the other word-categories are in the subject-
direct object form.

There are also special subject indicators, i.e. words which
serve to emphasize the subject. The pause (‖) after the word
functioning as subject also serves as a subject indicator.

4.2121. Subject indicators

A noun, pronoun, and any other part of speech mentioned in 4.212
may have a special subject indicator which emphasizes the subject;
cf. English I, for my part, ...

The subject indicators are always followed by a pause (‖).
The subject indicators are not obligatory when the subject is a

noun or a personal pronoun; in these cases the pause alone is
sufficient to point out the subject. They are, however, often
indispensable when the subject is an adjective, a demonstrative
pronoun, a numeral, or a verbal noun.

The following are subject indicators.

(1) /bolbəl/ or /bol/, e.g. /enə bol ‖ nom baenə/ 'this
is a book'.

(2) /gegči/, e.g. /arəd+tumən gegči ‖ tuməniig buteegči
xuči bilee/ 'the people's masses (/arəd+tumən/) are a force of
thousandfold creativity' (lit. 'a force that creates ten
thousand').

(3) The possessive suffix of the third person, here de-
prived of its original function because the object in question
is no one's possession, e.g. /əndərni ‖ gučiŋ aldə/ 'its depth
[is] thirty fathoms'; /abxən ‖ bexiidəg, əgəxən ‖ gediidəg/
'the one who takes usually bends forwards, the one who gives
usually bends backwards'; /xoyərni ‖ daxətae, xoyərni ‖ daxəgui/
'two of them [are] with fur coats, two of them [are] without
fur coats' (a riddle which means the ears and horns of the cow);
/sursənin ‖ dalae, suraagwini ‖ balae/ 'the one who has learned
[is] a sea, the one who did not learn [is] blind'.

(4) Short genitive forms of the personal pronouns, e.g.
/terə moritoe irdəgčin ‖ xeŋ bee/ 'who is that comer-of-thine
with the horse?'; /oləŋ čonə aləsəŋ ančincin ‖ ali bee/ 'which
is thy hunter who has killed many wolves?'.

4.2122. The pause

The pause (‖) is in many cases an indispensable mark of the
subject. It always follows the subject indicator; the pause
alone is, however, a sufficient subject indicator.

(1) After a noun immediately followed by another noun
which is not the subject, e.g. /altə ‖ məngənees wnətee baenə/
'gold is more expensive (or valuable) than silver' (without a
pause: /altə məngənees wnətee baenə/ '[it] is more expensive
than gold and/or silver'); /anči ‖ xwnees asuujee/ 'the hunter

154

asked the man' (without a pause: /aŋči xɯnees asuujee/ '[he]
asked the hunter', lit. 'the hunter man'); /togoo ‖ cae čanəbə/
'Togoo (a man's name) boiled tea' (without a pause: /togoo cae
čanəbə/ '[he] boiled a kettle of tea' -- /togoo/ 'kettle' is also
a personal name).

    (2) After a demonstrative pronoun, e.g. /enə ‖ nom/ 'this
[is] a book' (without a pause: /enə nom/ 'this book').

    (3) After a substantivized adjective, e.g. /tɯrgəŋ ‖
tɯɯxii, udaaŋ ‖ daamae/ 'fast [is] raw, slow [is] solid' (the
meaning of this saying is that things done in a hurry are of
poor quality whereas things done slowly are good); /xarə ‖
cagaaŋ biši/ 'black [is] not white'; /ulaaŋ ‖ šarə biši/ 'red
is not yellow' (without a pause: /ulaaŋ šarə biši/ '[it] is not
reddish-yellow').

    (4) After a numeral, e.g. /tabəŋ tabə ‖ xoriŋ tabə/ 'five
times five [is] twenty-five'.

    (5) After a verbal noun, e.g. /sursəŋ ‖ dalae, suraagɯi ‖
balae/ 'he who has learned [is] a sea, he who has not learned
[is] blind'.

4.21221. The pause may be very short or even completely lacking
only in a few cases.

    (1) When the clause is very short and the subject (a noun)
is immediately followed by a verbal predicate, e.g. /temee
bilčij yabənə/ 'a camel is grazing' (lit. 'walks grazing');
/ʒurəgčiŋ irəjee/ 'the photographer has come'.

    (2) After a personal pronoun, especially in short clauses
and in cases in which the pronoun is immediately followed by
the verb or an adverb, e.g. /ta xeʒee irsəŋ yum/ 'when did you
come?'.

4.213. <u>Agreement between the subject and predicate</u>
The Mongolian verb has no personal endings: there is only one
form for all three persons. The only verbal forms which refer
to particular persons are the imperative forms.

(1) Imperative forms.

A. When the subject is a pronoun of the first person
singular or plural, the verb is in the voluntative form, e.g.
/bi odoo yabəyaa/ 'I shall now go!'; /bidə tanaedə margaadar
irəyee/ 'we shall come to you tomorrow!'.

B. When the subject is a pronoun of the second person
singular or plural, the verb is in the imperative, benedictive,
precative, or imperative of the future, e.g. /či irə/ 'you
come!', /ta irəgtəŋ/ 'you come, please!', /či ireeč/ 'oh, come
(thou) for heaven's sake!', /ta ireet/ 'oh, come (you) for
heaven's sake!', /ireeree/ 'come later!'.

C. When the subject is a pronoun of the third person, or
a noun, the verb is in the imperative of the third person, e.g.
/terə irəg/ 'let him come!', /surəgčid irəg/ 'may the students
come!'.

(2) Noun functioning as predicate.

A. Agreement in number occurs when the subject is a plural,
and the predicate denotes some category of people (e.g. vocation),
e.g. /minii duɯnər ‖ saeŋ surəgčid baenə/ 'my younger brothers
are good students'.

B. Agreement in number occurs when there are two or more
subjects and the predicate denotes a certain category of people,
e.g. /dorǰi damdiŋ xoyər ‖ oncə saeŋ surəgčid yum/ 'Dorji and
Damdin (lit. 'Dorji, Damdin, two') are excellent students' (lit.
'are exclusively good students'); /dorǰi damdiŋ xoyər ‖ emčid
baenə/ 'Dorji and Damdin are physicians'.

C. There is no necessary agreement in case between the
subject and predicate. A noun or pronoun functioning as a
predicate may be in the subject-direct object case (or nominative) or genitive, e.g. /manae xuɯ ‖ bagši baenə/ 'our son is
teacher' (the predicate is a subject-direct object form); /enə
nom ‖ minii baenə/ 'this book is mine' (the predicate is a
genitive); /enə nom ‖ dorǰiiŋ/ 'this book is Dorji's' (the
predicate is a genitive).

4.214. Types of intonation and clause-structure

There are three main types of clause intonation in accordance
with which clauses are classified. The three types are the
falling, rising, and level intonation.

Falling intonation ($^-$_) is characteristic of declarative
clauses. Rising intonation (_$^-$) is characteristic of interrogative clauses. Level intonation is characteristic of exclamatory clauses.

4.2141. Declarative clauses

The intonation is either falling or falling-level.

(1) Falling intonation. The pitch is higher at the beginning of the clause, and falls, on the stressed syllables of the
successive words, to a lower point on the stressed syllable of
the last word of the clause. This type of intonation indicates
that the clause is the last in the sentence. It may be called
the "period intonation". It is rendered as /./ in phonemic
transcription.

$^-$_   /bucəĵ xoešoo xarxədə bogdəiiŋ xɯree ilxəŋ./ 'when one
   $^-$_   turns back and looks, Bogdiin Khuree (former name of
      $^-$ Ulaanbaatar) is distinct[ly seen]'
         _

$^-$_   ./neg xaanəii xɯɯxəŋ bišɯɯ terčin./ 'she is a khan's
   $^-$_   daughter' (lit. 'is she not a khan's daughter?', a
      $^-$ rhetorical question)

(2) Falling-level intonation. The pitch is higher at the
beginning of the clause and falls but remains level. This type
indicates that a further clause is to follow in the sentence.
It may be called the "comma-intonation" and is rendered as /,/
in phonemic transcription.

$^-$_ _ _ _ _ /bogdɔiiŋ əndər uuləndə budəŋtae xurə tatənə,/ 'on
            the high Bogdo Uula (a mountain near Ulaanbaatar),
            rain with fog envelopes [everything]'.

This clause is the first part of a stanza of a poem. Its
continuation is the clause given under (1). The whole stanza
displays the following intonation pattern:

‾ ⎯ ⎯ ⎯‑‑/,/ ‾‑‑
             ‑
              ‾
            ‾‑/./

4.21411. The normal order of words is subject + predicate, e.g.
/guilsə bol ‖ negə ʒuil ǰimis məŋ/ 'the Siberian apricot
(Armeniaca Sibirica L. Lam.) is a fruit'. In careless speech,
this order may be reversed:

    ‾ ⎯ /asuuǰee maŋgəs/ 'the Mangus (a fabulous monster)
        asked'

4.21412. In negative clauses the word order and intonation type
are the same as in declarative clauses.

4.2142. Interrogative clauses

The intonation is either rising or rising-falling.

(1) Rising intonation is characteristic of clauses in
which the question concerns the predicate. Here, the predicate
always takes the interrogative particle /uu/. In negative
interrogative clauses the predicate takes the negative particle
/gui/, to which the interrogative particle /uu/ is added, both
particles usually merging to /guyuu/. The intonation is rising,
with the high pitch on the last stressed syllable.

    ⎯‾/bagši irsənuu/ 'has the teacher come?'; /bagši
      irsəŋguyuu/ 'has the teacher not come?'

(2) Rising-falling intonation is characteristic of clauses
which contain an interrogative word, e.g. /xeŋ/ 'who?', /xaanə/
'where?', etc. In such clauses the question does not refer to
the predicate. A non-verbal predicate, i.e. a predicate which
is a noun or a verbal noun, and has no copula, takes the particle /be/ when the predicate ends in a consonant, or /b/ when
the predicate ends in a vowel. When used emphatically, /be/
becomes /bee/. Actually this /be/ or /b/ acts as a copula.
In such clauses the pitch is high on the stressed syllable of
the interrogative word and falls towards the predicate.

_ ⁻ _ /tanaedə xeŋ irsəŋ+be/ 'who has come to you?'

_ ⁻ - _/dorǰi yamər nom absəŋ⏐be/ 'what book has Dorji taken?'

4.2143. Exclamatory clauses

The pitch remains level on all stressed syllables, and the stress is stronger than usual.

_ _ _ /či bitəgii yabə/ 'do not go!'

_ _ _ /yaasəŋ xaluuŋ yum bee/ 'what heat!'

The normal order, complement + predicate, may be reversed in exclamatory clauses, the emphasis being on the elements at the beginning, e.g.:

_ _ /ir naašaa/ 'come here!' (in normal speech /naašaa ir/)

_ _ /ab tɯɯniig/ 'take it!' (in normal speech /tɯɯniig ab/)

4.22. Minor clauses

Minor (or fragmentary) clauses are characteristic of dialogues. Considered separately, they are often meaningless, but they supplement each other in the dialogue, e.g. /xɯɯxədiiŋ naer ‖ ənee bilɯɯ ‖ geǰi gombəruugaa xarəbə, gombən ‖ xaanaas daa, margaaši bišɯɯ./ 'Is the children's festival today?,' thus asking, he looked in Gombo's direction. Gombo [answered], 'Where (did you get this information)? [It's] tomorrow, is'nt it?'; /gombə irsənɯɯ? ɯgɯi. xeʒee irxəb? nəgeedər./ 'Has Gombo come?--No.--When will he come?--The day after tomorrow'.

4.23. Combination of clauses

There are two types: co-ordinate and subordinate clauses.

4.231. Co-ordination

Mongolian has only clauses with one syntactical predicate and one or several gerundial phrases, but no co-ordinate clauses of the English or Latin type. The gerunds in question are the imperfect gerund, the modal gerund, or the perfect gerund.

/asər udəlgui ‖ šənə xetəreed ‖ altəŋ nar ‖ ʒuuiŋ ʒugees
mandəǰi ‖ alibaag giiguuleed ‖ margaaši bolnə/ 'very
soon night will be over, the golden sun will rise in the
east and illuminate everything, and it will be tomorrow'
(lit. 'night having gone beyond the limits (/xetər-/
'to go beyond the limits'), the golden sun, rising from
the eastern side, having illuminated everything, tomorrow
becomes')

/xarəŋxui šənə əŋgərči ‖ xar uuiltə teŋgər ‖ xayaanaasaa
gegeerəbə/ 'dark night ended and the sky covered with
black clouds brightened on the horizon' (lit. 'dark night
ending, the sky with the black clouds brightened from its
edge')

/terə ʒam ‖ ulaaŋ narnəii urgəǰi gardəg ʒuuiŋ ʒug ‖ ʒaxə
xiaʒəgaargui alsədə uurgəlǰiləŋ ‖ uuinees əərə ʒam
baetəgae ‖ ǰimč uil uʒəgdənə/ 'that road continues in
the limitless distance in the eastern direction where
the red sun rises, [and] not only no road other than
this but not even a trail is to be seen' (lit. 'that
road continuing in the distance without edge or limit
in the eastern direction where the red sun always rises,
not only no road other than this but not even a trail is
seen')

/teŋgəriiŋ odə ‖ očišig gialəlʒaad, uul nuruug buurxəsəŋ
xuŋgər casənəii xasəiiŋ əngə ‖ tuuinii gerəldə alməsəiiŋ
adil gialtəgənə/ 'a star in the sky started glittering
like a spark, and the jade-like color of the snow-drifts
which had covered the mountain range gleamed in its
light like diamonds' (lit. 'a star of the sky, having
glittered like a spark, the jade's color of the snow-
drifts that had covered the mountain range gleamed in
its light like diamonds')

4.2311. In the literary language, clauses are linked to each other
by means of the conjunctions /begeed/ and /xiigeed/, which are

borrowings from Script Mongolian. The predicate of the whole
clause is a finite verb. The predicate of the preceding clause
is a verbal noun, followed by /bəgeed/ or /xiigeed/. These conjunctions are gerunds in origin, namely, /bəgeed/ < *bügeed,
perf. ger. of *bü- 'to be'; /xiigeed/ is the perf. ger. of
/xii-/ 'to do'. Consequently, phrases like /irsəŋ bəgeed/ are
translated literally as 'having been one who came'. As for
phrases like /irsəŋ xiigeed/, the literal translation is 'having
done the past coming'; in other words, these are gerundial phrases.

> /yamaanəii orilxə duu ‖ uləm uləm xoldəsoor ‖ čimee tasərsəŋ
> bəgeed ‖ naedəŋ araexiiŋ xoninəii əmnə garči togtəbə/ 'the
> screams of the goat were becoming more and more distant,
> sounds stopped, and Naedan went, with difficulty, and
> stood in front of the sheep' (lit. 'while the screaming
> voice of the goat became continuously more and more dis-
> tant, the sound stopped, and Naedan, with difficulty,
> coming out, stopped in front of the sheep')

> /buigədə naerəmdəxə moŋgəl arəd ulsəiig tuŋxəgləsəŋ xiigeed ‖
> aŋxədəgaar undəsəŋ xuuliig batəlsəŋ/ 'they proclaimed the
> Mongolian People's Republic, and ratified the first con-
> stitution (/undəsəŋ xuuli/, lit. 'basic law')'

4.2312. In the literary language, the conjunction /ba/, borrowed
from Script Mongolian, is also used.

> /duigrəgni ‖ usənəii oerə baexə ba, negee gonʒəgoeni ‖
> tuinees jaaxəŋ caanə ‖ naluu xajuudə baenə/ 'the circle
> is near the water, and the other oval is a little farther
> behind it and on the sloping side'

4.2313. What the native Mongolian grammarians call "co-ordinate
clauses without conjunctions" is simply a series of short
clauses, each with its own subject and predicate. There is no
reason for regarding such sentences as co-ordinate clauses.

> /yabəxə zam ‖ melciiŋ celgər saexəŋ, namərəiiŋ uiyəs tul ‖
> əbəsnii tolgoe naegənə/ 'The road he walks is even, wide,

beautiful. Because it is autumn time, the tops of the
grass swing.'

/bayəŋ bolədəiiŋ nasən ‖ dečeed, nɯdən ulbər, ʒaŋni təb
bolbəč ‖ ʒalin yixə boləltoe/ 'Bayan Bolod's age [is]
approximately forty. His eyes [are] reddish. Although
his character is calm, his slyness is probably great.'

4.232. Subordination

Mongolian does not have subordinate clauses but only subordinate
phrases. These are the verbal noun phrases and the gerundial
phrases; see 4.153(5,8).

4.2321. Quotation

(1) Direct quotation is usually inserted between the subject and the predicate of the whole clause. The predicate is a
form of the verb /ge-/ 'to say, to speak'.

/ecəgən ‖ xɯɯgiiŋ tolgoeg iləj ‖ yixə sergələŋ uxaantae
xɯɯxəd ‖ erdəm nom saeŋ surnə gebə/ 'His father,
stroking the son's head, said: "Very clever children
study well!" (lit. 'children with a very keen intellect study science (/erdəm nom/) well')'

(2) In clauses in which the predicate is not a form of the
verb /ge-/ but another verb, the quotation is linked to the
predicate by means of the imperfect gerund of the verb /ge-/,
i.e. /geji/ 'saying'.

/batə nadaas ‖ či enə noməiig uŋšisənuu gej asuubə/
'Bata asked me: "Have you read this book?" (lit.
'asked me saying')'

(3) Indirect quotation differs from direct only in that
the person addressed in the direct quotation appears in the
accusative form.

/noyəŋ tɯɯniig ir geji ʒaxirsəŋ/ 'the prince ordered
him to come (lit. 'The prince ordered, saying [about]
him: "Come!")'

/batə namaeg enə noməiig uŋšisənuu gej asuubə/ 'Bata
asked me whether I had read this book' (lit. 'Bata
asked saying [about] me "Has he read this book?")'

4.3. Select Bibliography

Bertagaev, T.A., Sintaksis sovremennogo mongol'skogo yazïka v
sravnitel'nom osveščenii, Prostoe predloženie, Moskva, 1964.

Luvsanvandan, S., Mongol xèlniĭ zǘin surax bičig, Dèd dèvtèr,
Ügüülbèriĭn zǘ, Ulaan Baatar, 1956.

Orčin cagiĭn mongol xèl zǘ, Ulaan Baatar, 1966.

Street, John C., Khalkha Structure, Bloomington, Indiana, 1963.

5. LITERATURE

Writing in the modern literary language based on the Khalkha dialect began in 1941. Until then, the old Written Mongolian (or Script Mongolian) language was used. Both the modern and the old literature show the influence of folklore, especially in the case of poetry.

5.1. Poetry

The characteristic features of Mongolian poetry are alliteration and parallelism. The typical Mongolian verse consists of a quatrain, i.e. a stanza of four lines, each of which consists of an equal number of syllables (usually seven or eight). Each line of a quatrain begins with the same syllable. The parallelism manifests itself in the repetition of the same idea, utilizing different expressions. These two principles underlie both the modern and the ancient poetry, the oldest specimens of which date from the thirteenth century. The following examples will illustrate the poetic forms described above:

A. Ancient poetry (Saγang Sečen, 1662):

arban nasutai daγaluγai bi
aliya maγui-ban ese uqaγdaluγai
arajan-dur dašiγuraγsan minu ünen bülüge
alus buruγu sanaγsan ügei bolai

qorin nasutai daγaluγai bi
qolčirqan maγu-ban ese medegdelügei
qorojan-dur dašiγuraγsan minu ünen bülüge
qoortu sedkil bariγsan ügei bolai

I followed [you] at the age of ten.

I have not been known [to play] any pranks.

It is true that I have become addicted to araǰa-liquor,

[However] I have had no far-reaching wrong ideas.

I followed [you] at the age of twenty.

I have not been known [to do] light-minded or evil things.

It is true that I have become addicted to qoroǰa-liquor,

[But] I have not conceived evil thoughts.

B. Modern poetry (Nacagdorǰ, 1923):

cènxèrlènxèn xaragdanaa xöö

cècèg navčtai uul bainaa xöö

čin zorigiig barival xöö

cèngèǰ bolmoor uul bainaa xöö

alaglanxan xaragdanaa xöö

aliɯ ǰiɯstèi uul bainaa xöö

amrag xoyor ürtèigèè xöö

am'darč bolmoor uul bainaa xöö

It is seen light blue,

It is a mountain [grown over] with flowers and foliage.

If we make a strong decision,

It will be a mountain where one might be happy.

It is seen multi-colored,

It is a mountain [grown over] with apple trees and berries.

It is a mountain where we might be able

To make our living, together, with our beloved children.

Mongolian folklore is very extensive, and includes songs, riddles, proverbs, tales, and epic sagas. The sagas are particularly characteristic of Mongolian folklore, and are still found

in the Mongolian People's Republic, especially in the Northwest
(inhabited by the Oirats). The Buriats also have very beautiful
epics. The epic sagas (ülgèr) are comprised of stories about
ancient heroes and their exploits and battles against enemies who
are either foreign kings or many-headed monsters, the so-called
mangas. The sagas always end happily. The hero may be defeated
or even be killed by the enemy at the beginning, but later he is
revived by a beautiful heavenly maiden and ultimately destroys
his enemy and marries the maiden. The ülgèr sometimes reach the
length of 20,000 verses (lines), each containing from five to
eight syllables, with only each two adjacent lines alliterating,
e.g.:

 xèntèĭ xaanï coxioo baĭxad

 xèrlèn tuulïg šalbaag baĭxad

 dalaĭ lamïg bandi baĭxad

 dayan xaanï balčir baĭxad

 xangaĭn modïg zulzag baĭxad

 xatan xarïg unag baĭxad

When [the mountain range] Khentei Khaan was a [single] cliff,

When [the rivers] Kherlen and Tuula were puddles,

When Dalai Lama was a novice,

When [the king] Dayan Khaan was an infant,

When the Khangai forest was a shoot,

When [the steed] Khatan Khara was a foal ...

The general significance of this excerpt is the depiction of the
concept of "a long time ago," when one of the largest mountain
ranges in Mongolia was still a single cliff, etc.

 The folk songs can be roughly classified into love songs,
songs about the beauty of nature, songs about horses, historical
songs, and religious songs, both shamanist and Buddhist.

 The riddles and proverbs reflect the life of the Buddhist
nomad society.

LITERATURE

A. Riddles:

"Four people have come from the north. Two of them have
fur coats, two of them have no coats." (Ears and horns
of a cow.)

"You go there, I go here, and we shall meet at the prince's
door." (A rope put around a nomad tent in order to pre-
vent the felt cover from being blown off by the wind.)

"An elegantly dressed gentleman without tinderbox and
tobacco." (Statue of Buddha.)

B. Proverbs:

"The more a man suffers, the more intelligent he becomes;
the more a pearl is rubbed, the more splendor it
acquires."

"A good man's word is food for a whole month; an evil man's
word is an obstacle for a whole day."

"One cannot wear a coat that is without [thread made of]
tendons; one cannot eat a soup that is without meat."

"The foremost wealth is virtue and knowledge; the medium
wealth is youthfulness; the very last wealth is cattle."

"One does not throw water at his ongon (i.e. idol, image of
a shamanist spirit); one does not curse his own clan."

5.2. The old literature

The oldest work of Mongolian literature is the so-called Secret
History, which represents a semi-legendary history of Chingis
Khan and his ancestors. It was probably written in 1240, although some scholars believe that it might have been compiled
twenty-four years later. It was originally written in Script
Mongolian and with the letters of the old alphabet, but later,
in the fourteenth century, a text in phonetic transcription,
with Chinese characters, was prepared which has been preserved,

although the original version has not survived. The Secret History is an important literary and historical work. Its text is interspersed with verses which are the oldest specimens of Mongolian poetry. The narration begins with an account of the legendary ancestors of Chingis Khan, the Grey Wolf and the Fair Doe, and proceeds to Chingis Khan's birth, and describes the hardships suffered by him in his childhood and youth, the organizing of his army, and the foundation of the Empire, and ends with the beginning of the reign of Chingis Khan's successor, his son Ögedei. The Secret History is an anonymous work, but some scholars believe that Chingis Khan's law-maker, Šiki Qutuγu, was the author.

Another specimen of the old literature is a song written on birch bark, which was found in 1930 during construction work in the Volga region in the USSR. It dates from the first half of the fourteenth century. The song represents a dialogue between a mother, who deplores the fact that her son has to leave and go to his lord, and her son, who tries to console her. To the same period also belong Buddhist verses carved on the walls of the Chü-yung-kuan Gate in China (1345). The verses praise the virtues of Emperor Khubilai (1259-1294), who "beautifully decorated the world with pagodas." This text, known as the Chü-yung-kuan Inscription, is written in the 'Phags-pa Script.

Historiography is the outstanding genre of old Mongolian literature. The oldest among the historical works is the Arban buyan-tu nom-un čaγan teüke (The White Chronicle of the Doctrine Endowed with Ten Meritorious Deeds), which goes back to the thirteenth century and represents, in part, a kind of state philosophy, in the center of which stands the theme of harmony between religion and worldly power.

A well-known historical work is the Erdeni-yin tobči (The Precious Button) by Saγang Sečen (1662), which is based on older Mongolian works, such as Šira tuγuji (The Yellow History), which, inter alia, contains genealogies. The author also used Chinese

and Tibetan sources. The chronicle begins with the creation of
the world, gives a history of ancient India and Tibet and a short
history of Buddhism, but the larger portion of the work is devoted to the history of the Mongols from the time of Chingis
Khan's legendary ancestor, the Grey Wolf, to the middle of the
seventeenth century. Another important historical work is Altan
tobči (The Golden Button) by Lubsan Danjin (written about 1655).
It also begins with a brief history of Indian and Tibetan kings,
and then proceeds to the history of the Mongols, from Chingis
Khan's ancestors to the downfall of the Khan Legden and the
Manchu conquest of Inner Mongolia in 1635. A work particularly
important for the history of Khalkha is Erdeni-yin erike (The
Precious Rosary) by Galdan, who was an aide to one of the Khalkha
princes. It was written in the 1860's. The most recent among
the historical works written in Script Mongolian is Mongγol-un
teüke by Amur, which was published in Ulanbator in 1930. It is
the first native history of Mongolia written in the manner of
Western historiography. The author discusses the Huns, Sien-pi,
Turks, and other predecessors of the Mongols and ends the book
with the Yüan dynasty.

The old literature abounds in epic works. One that is
widely known is "The Destroyer of the Roots of Ten Evils in
Ten Regions, The Holy Geser Khan." Although of Tibetan origin,
the Geser Khan sagas are spread among all Mongols, Buriats, and
Oirats. The Script Mongolian version was published as a xylograph in Peking in 1716, and was set in type and reproduced in
St. Petersburg in 1836 by I.J. Schmidt, who also made a German
translation. This edition contains seven of the original fifteen
sagas. The first saga is the story of Geser Khan's miraculous
birth and his childhood pranks; the remaining six describe his
heroic exploits. Another large epic work is Qan Qarangγui
(Prince Kharangui) which is, in form, closer to the oral ülger
sagas. The main character of a number of epics is Chingis Khan,
e.g. "The Tale About the Two Horses of Chingis Khan," in which
we learn that Chingis Khan did not pay much attention to his two

horses, who felt hurt and left him, but soon found out that separation from their lord and master was too high a price for freedom, and so they went back to him. Chingis Khan recognized them, and when he went hunting he rode one of these steeds, which drew great admiration from all people. The other steed was dedicated to the gods.

Some tales about Chingis Khan are gnomic in character. Such is the "Admonitions of Chingis Khan, for His Younger Brothers and Sons," in which Chingis Khan appears as a wise man, and asks his brothers and sons questions, such as: "What is the greatest happiness?" All their answers are wrong, e.g. that of Chaghatai: "The greatest happiness is to destroy the enemies, to vanquish a horseman, to separate two people engaged to each other, and to bring booty." Chingis Khan explains that this is childish happiness, the greatest happiness being bringing prosperity to the nation, keeping the affairs of state in good order, bringing peace to the people, particularly to the younger generation.

The old literature also contains many works translated from other languages. Thus, the Pañcatantra fables were translated from a Tibetan text, which was, in its turn, translated from Sanskrit. Similarly, the stories of King Vikramāditya, Kisana (Kṛṣṇa), and the "Tales of the Magic Vampire" are of Indic origin.

The vast Buddhist literature is also, to a great extent, of Indic origin. Such are the so-called Jātaka or birth-stories and tales about the previous lives of Buddha. The Buddhist philosophical and religious works go back to Sanskrit originals, although most of them were translated from Tibetan into Mongolian. The Buddhist canon, the so-called Tripitaka (in Sanskrit) or Kanjur (in Tibetan and Mongolian), which consists of 108 large volumes, was translated into Mongolian in the seventeenth century and published in xylograph in 1720. The Buddhist encyclopedia, the so-called Tanjur, in 225 volumes, was published in 1741.

Some literary works were translated from Chinese, such as novels and stories, e.g. the historical adventure novels, "The Tale of Three Nations," "Journey to the West," etc.

The Mongols first became acquainted with Russian and European literature at the beginning of the present century. The Mongolian writer and scholar, Tseven Jamtsarano (1888-1940?) started, in 1911 in Urga (now Ulanbator), the newspaper Neyislel küriyen-ü sonin (News of the Capital) and the magazine Šine toli (The New Mirror), in which short stories translated from other languages and information about current world affairs appeared. He also translated the historical novel La bannière bleue (1877) by Léon Cahun, and a few minor writings of Leo Tolstoi.

After 1921, when the Mongolian Learned Committee (present Academy of Sciences) was founded, literary activities increased considerably.

5.3. The modern literature

The birth of modern poetry is connected with the name of Nacagdorǰ (1906-1937), who put new content into the traditional forms of Mongolian poetry. Preserving the alliteration, parallelism, and the quatrain, he devoted his verses to the new Mongolia. One of his poems is "The Song of the Pioneers [revolutionary boy scouts]." Other poems describe his travels ("From Ulanbator to Berlin") or are devoted to young people traveling abroad in order to study ("One Who Travels to Study Abroad"), to students ("Our Students"), or to working-people ("Woman-Servant"). Children are the subject of some poems ("May There Be Many Mongolian Children!"). He has also written lyric poems, such as "Spring," "Summer," "The Hindu Dancer," etc.

Nacagdorǰ also wrote plays and short stories. Modern prose was founded, however, by Damdinsüren (1908-), a prominent scholar, poet, and writer. His novel Gologdoson xüüxèn (The Rejected Girl) is the first native Mongolian work to deal with problems of real life. This novel is about a young girl, daughter of a poor family, who has no opportunity in her native place. She is given, against her will, in marriage to a rich man. One day she meets a woman from town who tells her about the rights of women in post-Revolutionary Mongolia. She leaves her home and goes to Ulanbator, enters a school, and thus starts an independent life.

Damdinsüren is also known as the author of numerous short stories, and as the most outstanding poet of Mongolia at the present time.

Another well-known writer is Rinchen (1905-), who is also a well-known scholar. His most famous work is <u>Üüriĭn tuyaa</u> (The Beam of Dawn), a novel devoted to the struggle of the Mongols for liberation from foreign domination and for independence. It occupies in the history of Mongolian literature a place comparable to Leo Tolstoi's <u>War and Peace</u>. Another literary work of his is <u>Zaan Zaluudaĭ</u>, the story of a prehistorical man and his struggle for survival. An interesting and well-written account of his sojourn in Europe is his "Notes on Travel in the West, My Journey in Hungary."

Other popular writers are Biamba, Erdene, Baast, Darǰaa, Nadmid, and Perlee. Lodoidamba is the author of several novels. The main characters of his novel "In the Altai Mountains" are geologists. His other novel, "The Clear Tamir River," is about paupers in ancient times and their tragic fates.

A psychological novel is <u>Cag töriĭn üĭmeen</u> (Upheaval), by Namdag. It depicts the inner conflict and spiritual awakening of a government official.

Well-known poets are Gaitav (1929-), and Yavuuxulan (1929-). Authors of plays are Čimid, Lodoidamba, Oidov, Oyuun, and Vangan.

5.4. <u>Select bibliography</u>

Bawden, C.R., <u>Vikramāditya Tales from Mongolia</u> (= <u>Mongol-Pitaka,</u> <u>being the Mongolian Collectanea in the series of Indo-Asian</u> <u>Literature forming the Śatapitaka</u>, vol. 6), New Delhi, 1962. [Mongolian text with a brief résumé of contents.]

-----, <u>Tales of King Vikramāditya and the Thirty-Two Wooden Men</u>, New Delhi, 1960. [Translation.]

172

LITERATURE

-----, The Mongol Chronicle Altan Tobči: Text, translation, and critical notes (= Göttinger Asiatische Forschungen, vol. 5), Wiesbaden, 1955.

Damdinsüren, C., Tüüvèr zoxiol, Ulaanbaatar, 1956. [Biography and his works, in Mongolian.]

Gerasimovič, L.K., Literatura Mongol'skoǐ Narodnoǐ Respubliki 1921-1964 godov, Leningrad, 1965. [History of modern Mongolian literature.]

Haenisch, E., Die Geheime Geschichte der Mongolen: Aus einer mongolischen Niederschrift des Jahres 1240 von der Insel Kode'e im Keluren-Fluss, Erstmalig übersetzt und erläutert, Zweite verbesserte Auflage, Leipzig, 1948. [German translation of the Secret History.]

Heissig, W., Die Familien- und Kirchengeschichtsschreibung der Mongolen: I, 16.-18. Jahrhundert (= Asiatische Forschungen, vol. 5), Wiesbaden, 1959. [An important work on Mongolian chronicles of the 16th-18th centuries.]

-----, Helden-, Höllenfahrts- und Schelmengeschichten: Aus dem Mongolischen übersetzt, Manesse-Verlag, Zürich, 1962.

-----, Mongolische Volksmärchen: Aus dem Mongolischen übersetzt und mit einem Nachwort, Eugen Diederichs Verlag, Düsseldorf-Köln, 1963.

Jülg, B., Mongolische Märchen-Sammlung: Die neun Märchen des Siddhi-Kür und die Geschichte des Ardschi-Bordschi Chan, Innsbruck, 1868. [Mongolian text and German translation of nine tales of the "Magic Vampire" and part of the "Arji Borji Story," which is close to Vikramāditya.]

Krueger, J.R., Poetical Passages in the Erdeni-yin Tobči: A Mongolian Chronicle of the Year 1662, by Saγang Secen, Mouton and Co., S'-Gravenhage, 1961.

-----, Sagang Sechen, Prince of the Ordos Mongols, The Bejewelled Summary of the Origin of the Khans (Qad-un ündüsün-ü erdeni-yin tobci), A History of the Eastern Mongols to 1662, Part One: Chapters One through Five, From the Creation of the World to the Death of Genghis Khan (1227), Newly translated from the original Mongolian, Second edition, (= The Mongolia Society Occasional Papers, No. 2), Bloomington, Indiana, 1967.

Laufer, B., "Skizze der mongolischen Literatur", Keleti Szemle-Revue Orientale, vol. VIII, Budapest, 1907, pp. 165-261. [A general outline of Mongolian folklore and old literature. There is a revised and supplemented Russian translation; see B. Laufer, Očerk mongol'skoǐ literaturi, Perevod V. A.

Kazakeviča, pod redakcieĭ i s predisloviem B. Ya. Vladimircova, Leningrad, 1927.]

Loewenthal, R. see Žamcarano, C.Ž.

Mostaert C.I.C.M., Antoine, Folklore ordos (Traduction des textes oraux ordos) (= Monumenta Serica, Monograph XI), Peiping, 1947. [French translation of a large number of songs, proverbs, riddles, and tales collected among the Ordos Mongols.]

Nacagdorǰ, D., Zoxioluud, Ulaanbaatar, 1961. [Nacagdorǰ's works, with a biography by B. Sodnom, in Mongolian.]

Pelliot, P., Histoire secrète des Mongols: Restitution du texte mongol et traduction française des chapitres I à VI, Paris, 1949.

Poppe, N., Xalxa-mongol'skiĭ geroičeskiĭ èpos, Moskva-Leningrad, 1937. [A general work on the Mongolian epic sagas, their contents, form, poetical aspects, etc.]

-----, Mongolische Volksdichtung, Sprüche, Lieder, Märchen und Heldensagen: Khalkha-mongolische Texte mit Übersetzung und Anmerkungen, Wiesbaden, 1955. [Mongolian sagas, tales, songs, etc., with German translation.]

-----, "Der Parallelismus in der epischen Dichtung der Mongolen", Ural-Altaische Jahrbücher, vol. 30 (1958), pp. 195-228.

-----, "Zur Hyperbel in der epischen Dichtung der Mongolen", Zeitschrift der Deutschen Morgenländischen Gesellschaft, vol. 112 (1962), pp. 104-158.

-----, "The Mongolian Versions of the Vessantarajātaka", (= Studia Orientalia, edidit Societas Orientalis Fennica XXX:2), 1964. [Mongolian and Oirat text and translation of one of the well-known birth-stories.]

-----, The Twelve Deeds of Buddha, A Mongolian Version of the Lalitavistara: Mongolian Text, Notes, and English Translation (= Asiatische Forschungen, vol. 23), Wiesbaden, 1967. [Part of a Buddha biography.]

-----, The Mongolian Monuments in ḥP'ags-pa Script, Second edition, translated and edited by John R. Krueger (= Göttinger Asiatische Forschungen, vol. 8), Wiesbaden, 1957. [On pp. 60-66 the Buddhist verses from the Chü-yung-kuan gate.]

-----, "Zolotoordïnskaja rukopis' na bereste", Sovetskoe Vostoko-vedenie II, Moskva-Leningrad, 1941, pp. 81-136. [The manuscript

on birch bark, the Mongolian text and a Russian translation
of the fragments.]

Rinčen, B., Üüriĭn tuyaa, I-II, Ulaanbaatar, 1951; III, Ulaanbaatar, 1955.

-----, Zaan Zaluudaĭ, Balar èrtniĭ tyyxèn roman, I, Ulaanbaatar,
1964; II, Ulaanbaatar, 1966.

-----, Baruun ètgèèd zorčson tèmdèglèl, Maĭar ulsaar yavsan min',
Ulaanbaatar, 1959.

Rupen, R.A., "Cyben Žamcaranovič Žamcarano (1880-?1940)", Harvard
Journal of Asiatic Studies, vol. 19, 1956, pp. 126-145.
[Biography and bibliography.]

Sanžeev, G.D., Mongol'skaya povest' o Xane Xarangue, Moskva-
Leningrad, 1937. [Mongolian text and Russian translation of
the saga Qan Qarangγui.]

Schmidt, I.J., Geschichte der Ost-Mongolen und ihres Fürstenhauses
verfasst von Ssanang Ssetsen Chungtaidschi der Ordus, St.
Petersburg und Leipzig, 1829. [The Mongolian text and German
translation of the Chronicle by Saγang Sečen, 1662.]

Sodnom, B., Dašdoržiĭn Nacagdoržiĭn namtar zoxiol, Ulaanbaatar,
1966. [Nacagdorj's biography and analysis of his poems, in
Mongolian.]

Vladimircov, B. Ya., Mongol'skiĭ sbornik razskazov iz Pañcatantra,
Petrograd, 1921. [The Mongolian text of the Pañcatantra, a
Russian translation, and notes. An important chapter on the
different periods of history of the Mongolian written language.]

-----, Mongolo-oĭratskiĭ geroičeskiĭ èpos, Petersburg-Moskva,
1923. [Russian translation of several epic sagas. An important introduction dealing with epics, bards, etc.]

Žamcarano, C.Ž., The Mongol Chronicles of the Seventeenth Century,
translated by Rudolf Loewenthal (= Göttinger Asiatische
Forschungen, vol. 3) Wiesbaden, 1955. [A general description
and analysis of several chronicles.]